The message of *Distinct Communion* has the potential to be life-transforming. In its pages, Dan Peters explains what many Christians intuitively sense but rarely articulate. If a nervous young minister or theological student begins to pray 'Our Father in heaven ...' and a moment later says 'thank you for dying for us on the cross', we cut him some slack: nervousness has confused his theology! We instinctively realize that we cannot praise the Father for dying for us— simply because he didn't. His Son died. Yet we rarely reflect on the implications of this intuition—that if Father, Son and Spirit participate in distinctive ways in creation, providence, and redemption, then our communion with each person will also have its own unique elements.

In *Distinct Communion* Dan Peters joins a number of great theologians who have understood, expounded and applied this principle. Grasp its message and our individual and corporate experience of the privileges of fellowship with God will grow exponentially. And we will be thankful to Dan Peters for so clearly and thoughtfully introducing us to a biblical principle that has life-transforming implications.

SINCLAIR B. FERGUSON
Teaching Fellow, Ligonier Ministries

Dan Peters takes the piety of the early Church Father, Gregory of Nazianzus, as a springboard for contemplating and exploring the reality of the triune God. Gregory famously addressed God as "my Trinity". Yet too often the Trinitarian being and works of God have not occupied a central place in Evangelical piety or theology. In this book, Peters seeks to shepherd us back into the life-giving mystery of the Trinity, made known in the incarnation of the Son, which so pervades the pages of the New Testament. Readers will find here an abundance of stimulating material to aid them in appropriating God's blessed triune reality, and in nourishing a right and enriching relationship with Father, Son, and Holy Spirit, for His glory and our good.

NICK NEEDHAM
Church History Tutor, Highland Theological College
Dingwall, UK

DISTINCT
COMMUNION

The Believer's Relations with Father, Son, and Holy Spirit

DAN PETERS
Foreword by Ian Hamilton

MENTOR

Copyright © Dan Peters 2025

paperback ISBN 978-1-5271-1188-2
ebook ISBN 978-1-5271-1261-2

10 9 8 7 6 5 4 3 2 1

Published in 2025
Christian Focus Publications Ltd,
Geanies House, Fearn, Ross-shire,
IV20 1TW, Scotland.

www.christianfocus.com

Cover design by Reubner Durais

Printed and bound by Bell & Bain, Glasgow

To my parents,

Malcolm and Caroline,

who know and love the triune God.

Contents

Foreword

I count it a privilege to commend this book, brief in its length but profound in its subject matter. The title of the book is immediately compelling, *Distinct Communion: The Believer's Relations with Father, Son, & Holy Spirit.* The author describes it as a 'modest attempt' to engage with the profoundest subject a human being could ever engage with. It may be modest in its brevity, but the work is theologically rich, practically stimulating and engagingly written.

In his Introduction to Athanasius' great work, *On the Incarnation of the Word of God*, C.S. Lewis comments that for him the most significant devotional books have been the classic works on Christian theology. *Distinct Communion* is in the classic tradition of rich theology, but no less is it deeply devotional.

Dan Peters was my first pastoral assistant when I served as minister of Cambridge Presbyterian Church. He was a colleague whose preaching I always found heart-warming and theologically stimulating. Dan and his wife, Hannah, endeared themselves to our congregation and we missed them greatly when the Lord moved them on to new spheres of ministry.

Dan writes with theological insight into the deepest realities of God's revelation in Holy Scripture, the revelation of himself. Almost as impressive is the lucid, compelling prose that gives energy and beauty to the subject matter. As you read this book you are increasingly aware that the writer feels the weight and the glory of the *Distinct Communion* he is explicating. Dan not only writes out of Scripture, he writes out of his own experience of communion with God.

This is no abstract, dry theological study – how could it be when the subject is the all glorious Triune God! Sadly, however, there are books on the doctrine of God that read more like theological multiplication tables rather than heart-warming, mind-expanding, devotional enquiries into the ever-blessed, all glorious God, Father, Son and Holy Spirit. Thankfully, this study will stir your heart and compel your mind to explore the wonders of God and bring you to a fresh understanding of the essential trinitarian glory of Christianity.

Martin Bucer, the Strasbourg reformer who so deeply influenced John Calvin wrote, 'True theology is not theoretical, it is practical. The end of it is to live a godly life'. This conviction runs like a golden thread throughout Dan's exposition of the believer's distinct communion with the Persons of the Godhead. He helps us to understand that the doctrine of the Holy Trinity should not be a truth that Christians simply affirm and then ignore as having no practical value. On the contrary, there is no revealed truth of more practical significance for Christian living, worship, even evangelism, than the truth of God's triune being and the believer's distinct communion with Father, Son and Holy Spirit.

If eternal life is all about knowing God and Jesus Christ whom he sent (John 17:3), should not the Christian and the Christian church give themselves more than we presently do (even if I speak only for myself) to studying the great God 'from whom, through whom, and to whom, are all things. To him be glory' (Rom. 11:36)? I, for one, intend to recommend *Distinct Communion* wherever I go. Buy it. Read it. Be lifted into the heights by it. Truth is for living.

IAN HAMILTON
President of Westminster Seminary
Newcastle, UK

Introduction

I was an undergraduate at the time. I had read little, if anything, by John Owen. The phrase *distinct communion* would have meant nothing to me. But one sentence in a book on Christology managed to lodge itself into a compartment of my brain. The writer, Donald Macleod, was discussing the believer's communion with Christ. In that context he offered this remark: 'I have a relationship with him which I do not have with God the Father.'[1]

I suppose that, read by itself, the sentence could be misunderstood. It could give the impression that the believer has a relationship with Christ, but not much of a relationship with the Father. I suspect many Christians in the history of the church have harboured precisely that idea: Christ is warm and inviting; God the Father is cold and forbidding. That, however, was not what Macleod meant. His meaning was clarified a few pages later in the same book: 'We have an experience of each [divine person] which is different from

---

1. Donald Macleod, *The Person of Christ* (Leicester: Inter-Varsity Press, 1998), 138.

our experience of the other. There is an "Abba, Father!";
a "Lord Jesus!"; and a "Come, Holy Spirit!"[2]

For many years Macleod's sentence remained lodged but
undeveloped. I pondered it intermittently. I found the concept
of relating differently to Father, Son and Spirit logical, and I
found it attractive. But I did not find it woven into the fabric
of contemporary Christian piety. As far as I could see, it was
absent from the majority of songs and hymns, it was absent
from most public prayers, and it was absent from the many,
well-intentioned exhortations to 'pursue a close relationship
with God.' If it was true that the believer has a relationship
with Christ which she does not have with the Father, then
most believers seemed blithely unaware of it.

Eventually, however, my theological meanderings
landed me in the seventeenth century. And, suddenly,
that suggestive sentence, lying dormant in the back of my
mind, came into its own. I encountered writers in that era
whose Christian devotion was not one-dimensional; it was
three-dimensional. I discovered men who did not enjoy a
relationship with 'God'; they enjoyed relationships with the
Father, the Son and the Spirit.

In some of them it expressed itself in modest ways.
James Durham, whose work will be considered in chapter
6 of this book, falls into that category. But others wrote
effusively of relating to the different divine persons. One
such was Thomas Goodwin. His work on *Justifying Faith* is
a marvellous antidote to cold, rationalistic conceptions of
'believing in Jesus'. He argued there that the believer should
aspire to assurance; and he contended that assurance is 'not
only an assurance of the benefits that…are ours…but it is a
fellowship'; and he defined that fellowship as 'fellowship with
all the persons, Father, Son, and Holy Ghost, and their love,

2. Ibid., 142.

severally and distinctly.' He then over several pages issued an impassioned plea, only snatches of which can be quoted here:

> Do not then stint yourselves here, that it sufficeth that you know the Father. No; Christ putteth you upon labouring after a distinct knowing of, and communion with all three persons ... not only ... to have fellowship with the one in the other implicitly, but distinctly with the one and with the other, and distinctly with the one as with the other ... As the three angels that came to Abraham were all entertained by him, so for a man to converse with, and entertain into his heart...all three persons, and to have the love of them all distinctly brought home to his heart, and to view the love of them all apart, this is the communion that [the Scriptures] would raise up our hearts unto ... Sometimes a man's communion and converse is with the one, sometimes with the other; sometimes with the Father, then with the Son, and then with the Holy Ghost; sometimes his heart is drawn out to consider the Father's love in choosing, and then the love of Christ in redeeming, and so the love of the Holy Ghost, that searcheth the deep things of God, and revealeth them to us.[3]

But even with lines like those flowing from his pen, Goodwin was not the premier exponent of this theme. That accolade is reserved for John Owen. He wrote on Christian devotion in a very similar way to Goodwin: the words just quoted could easily be mistaken for Owen's. But whereas fellowship with Father, Son and Spirit elicited a few pages from Goodwin, it compelled a whole, weighty volume from Owen. Entitled *Of Communion with God the Father, Son, and Holy Ghost, Each Person Distinctly, in Love, Grace, and Consolation,* its

---

3. Thomas Goodwin, *The Object and Acts of Justifying Faith*, in *The Works of Thomas Goodwin* (Edinburgh: James Nichol, 1865), 8:377-379.

very structure is arresting: part one addresses communion with the Father, part two communion with the Son, and part three communion with the Spirit.

In these old divines I had found what had been tantalising me all those years. I had found the concept of *distinct communion*. Distinct communion is exactly what it sounds like. It is communing with each person of the Godhead in a way that is distinct. It is experiencing a relationship with each that is distinguishable from one's relationships with the others. These Puritan writers were convinced that this is the pattern to which healthy Christian devotion should conform.

It would be misleading to give the impression that *all* the Puritans felt that conviction. It is not the case that seventeenth-century piety was awash with distinct communion. Considering, indeed, how many works on the Christian's devotional life were spawned in that era, it is striking how seldomly the theme of distinct communion surfaces. The reason for that may partly be connected to an inherent weakness of the Puritan movement. Its keynote was experiential Christianity. It eschewed formalism. Heart-engagement with God was the great priority. This was laudable and refreshing, but was maintained to some degree at the expense of doctrinal rigour. The brightest stars in the Puritan galaxy, like Goodwin and (especially) Owen, were able to marry the devotional vitality of the day with the best Trinitarian theology of the past — and the result was distinct communion. Many others, however, were not. In their passion for knowing God, loving God and experiencing God, they overlooked the most basic truth about God: he is three persons, and can only be known, loved and experienced as such. As Brian Kay puts it:

The substantial trinitarian emphases of [earlier generations] often were inadequately translated in any sustained way to the otherwise elaborate Puritan devotional models. The doctrine of God was failing to connect to spirituality … The real weakness of some Puritan devotion is not that it was too doctrinal, but that it was not doctrinal enough.[4]

But there is more at play than just the failure of that era to combine devotion and doctrine. There is a bigger picture. The Puritan period represents one chapter within Western Christianity, and it is arguable that throughout the whole story there has been a reluctance to let God's tripersonality set the agenda for worship and communion. In the east the Cappadocian Fathers, delighting in 'the splendour of the three,'[5] set a trajectory that was conducive to distinct communion. But the trajectory set by Augustine in the west, with his emphasis on an indivisible divine essence, was less

---

4. Brian Kay, *Trinitarian Spirituality: John Owen and the Doctrine of God in Western Devotion* (Milton Keynes: Paternoster, 2007), 56-57. It is worth mentioning in passing another figure from that period, Samuel Rutherford. These beautiful words have been attributed to him: 'I know not which divine person I love the most, but this I know, I need and love each of them' (quoted in Joel R. Beeke, *Puritan Reformed Spirituality* [Grand Rapids, Michigan: Reformation Heritage Books, 2004], 435). I have never succeeded in locating this sentence in Rutherford's writings. On the assumption, however, that it is bona fide, it represents a particularly noteworthy exception to this seventeenth-century weakness I am highlighting. For Rutherford is the acme of experiential Christianity. His devotional material — especially in his letters — is at times unsettlingly intense. Yet these words, if his, indicate that this devotional intensity — his deeply felt need of and love for God — was controlled by a profound, clear-sighted Trinitarianism.

5. Gregory Nazianzen's words (Gregory Nazianzen, *Orations* 40.41, in *The Nicene and Post-Nicene Fathers*, vol. 7, ed. Philip Schaff and Henry Wace [Grand Rapids, Michigan: Wm. B. Eerdmans Publishing Company, 1978], 375.

conducive to it. Robert Letham identifies only two western figures who have significantly broken the mould. One is John Calvin; the other is John Owen.[6]

Owen's monumental work on *Communion with God* seems to be 'on the radar' of sections of the twenty-first-century church. Certainly, in scholarly circles it receives attention. This could suggest an overcoming of past reluctance, a burgeoning enjoyment of the splendour of the three. But is that really evident when one looks at our actual engagement with God today?

Singing occupies a prominent place in contemporary evangelical worship. A new generation of songwriters has gifted the church much material that is pleasingly substantial and biblical. Some of that material is at least moderately Trinitarian, making mention of the different divine persons. But few of these fresh compositions are serviceable for full-blown distinct communion with the Father, the Son and the Spirit.

Over the centuries a hymnic model has surfaced from time to time whereby the divine persons are addressed in

---

6. Robert Letham, *The Holy Trinity: In Scripture, History, Theology, and Worship* (Phillipsburg, N.J.: P&R Publishing, 2004), 408-409. It is possible that Letham overstates the case. Ryan McGraw contends that Owen 'shows affinity with Dutch authors such as Voetius and Hoornbeeck,' and that 'his emphasis on the persons of the Godhead stems from a continental influence.' But McGraw does acknowledge that 'Owen is largely unique among English writers in terms of Trinitarian piety.' Thus, while we should perhaps be cautious of giving 'the impression that western Trinitarians are the "bad guys"' (Ryan M. McGraw, 'The Rising Prominence of John Owen: A Review Article of *The Ashgate Research Companion to John Owen's Theology*,' *Mid-America Journal of Theology* 24 [2013]: 114), it is nonetheless true that Owen's distinct communion stands out as something striking and unusual within his tradition.

turn across consecutive verses. A fine example from Isaac Watts (1674–1748) is 'We Give Immortal Praise';[7] from Edward Cooper (1770-1833) there is 'Father of Heaven, Whose Love Profound'. More recently, Margaret Clarkson's 'Sing Praise to the Father, Creator and King' follows the same contours, as does Andrew Goddard's 'Heavenly Father, Our Creator.' The transitioning of the worshipper's gaze from one divine person to another does not have to be as formulaic as in these examples. But one wishes there were more songs being written today which, in one way or another, transport a congregation to the distinct enjoyment of the Glorious Three.

But it is not just our singing that can seem far removed from Owen's vision of communion. There are also the prayers offered during services of worship. Here, distinct communion can be hampered by the idea that the Father only is always to be addressed — through the Son and by the Spirit. In many cases, however, one encounters something even more inimical to tri-personal praise than that overly rigid model. Sheer *sloppiness* is the principal impediment! Prayers are fired off, prefaced by words like 'God' and 'Lord,' and it is simply unclear what the speaker has in mind: it could be a particular divine person; it could be the three

---

7. 'To Him Who Chose Us First,' also by Watts, similarly addresses the three persons, but the structure is a little subtler. It is ironic that it should be this particular writer who so successfully translates Owen's Trinitarian devotion into the realm of hymnody. Watts was one of Owen's successors to the pulpit of Mark Lane Independent Chapel, London, but, according to Crawford Gribben, 'moved away from the theological position which Owen had articulated, eventually proposing doctrine which encouraged Unitarians to believe he had endorsed their own position' (Crawford Gribben, 'Becoming John Owen: The Making of an Evangelical Reputation,' *Westminster Theological Journal* 79[2] [2017]: 313).

persons in their unity; or it could be that the triune being of God is not in fact conceived of at all in that moment.

While it is encouraging, then, that Owen's work is on the radar, our congregational engagement with God often betrays little of its influence. There is a great need for distinct communion to become less of a theological curiosity encased in a seventeenth-century text, and more of a weekly liturgical priority.

The book that is in your hands is not an analysis of that seventeenth-century text. Others have engaged closely with Owen's volume, and doubtless many more treatments of that kind will emerge in the future. This book is interested in distinct communion itself. Moving from some texts of Scripture to some theological principles, and then to some practical details, it is a modest attempt to concentrate minds on this great theme.

A.W. Tozer pens a vivid description of that enigmatic nineteenth-century figure, Frederick Faber. Faber is probably not an obvious role model for evangelical protestants! Nor am I able to verify that Tozer's image of the man corresponded to reality. But that aside, we can dwell on the attractiveness of the following lines, and covet for our own Christian lives something of what Tozer describes:

> [Faber's] love for God extended to the three Persons of the Godhead equally, yet he seemed to feel for each One a special kind of love reserved for Him alone. Of God the Father he sings: ... *Father of Jesus, love's reward! What rapture will it be, Prostrate before Thy throne to lie, And gaze and gaze on Thee!* His love for the Person of Christ was so intense it threatened to consume him.... Faber's blazing love extended also to the Holy Spirit.... He literally pressed his forehead to

the ground in his eager fervid worship of the Third Person of the Godhead.[8]

It is my hope and prayer that more of our churches might be filled with men and women whose love extends to the three persons equally, and who have a relationship with each that is distinct; and that this might increasingly be reflected in the way that we pray and sing together.

And on the subject of singing, no hymn could propel us into the following pages more appropriately than Edward Cooper's, mentioned above. With its eye on redemption *planned, accomplished* and *applied* — the relevance of which to distinct communion will emerge in later chapters — the song moves with non-discriminatory relish from *God the Father* to *God the Son* to *God the Spirit*!

> Father of heaven, whose love profound
> a ransom for our souls hath found,
> before thy throne we sinners bend,
> to us thy pardoning love extend.
>
> Almighty Son, incarnate Word,
> our Prophet, Priest, Redeemer, Lord,
> before thy throne we sinners bend,
> to us thy saving grace extend.
>
> Eternal Spirit, by whose breath
> the soul is raised from sin and death,
> before thy throne we sinners bend,
> to us thy quickening power extend.
>
> Thrice Holy! Father, Spirit, Son;
> mysterious Godhead, Three in One,
> before thy throne we sinners bend,
> grace, pardon, life to us extend.

---

8. A.W. Tozer, *The Pursuit of God* (Bromley: STL Books, 1981), 40-42.

PART 1

THE BIBLICAL FOUNDATIONS OF DISTINCT COMMUNION

CHAPTER ONE

The Language and Imagery of Communion

The purpose of this book is to explore the believer's communion with the distinct persons of the Godhead. But before entering the deep waters of Trinitarian theology we must address a more basic issue. What is communion with God? It is necessary to establish the meaning of this concept. Only then may we consider whether and how we experience it with different divine persons.

John Owen's treatment of communion has already been mentioned in the introduction, and its monumental status intimated. One sentence in the opening pages of that work is (with good reason) often quoted. Communion with God, Owen says, 'consisteth in his communication of himself unto us, with our returnal unto him of that which he requireth and accepteth, flowing from that union which in Jesus Christ we have with him.'[1]

---

1. John Owen, *Of Communion with God the Father, Son, and Holy Ghost, Each Person Distinctly, in Love, Grace, and Consolation* (1657), in *The Works of John Owen*, ed. William H. Goold (Edinburgh: Banner of Truth, 2004), 2:8-9.

That definition contains a crucial distinction. By distinguishing *communion* from *union*, Owen directs our thoughts to a particular dimension of the believer's relationship with God. *Union* (with Christ) signifies the fixed, static dimension of the relationship. It remains constantly intact, irrespective of moral, emotional and circumstantial vicissitudes. *Communion*, Owen says, is not that. It flows from it, but is different. It is the dynamic, variable dimension of the believer's relationship with God. Whereas *union* is about the existence of the relationship, *communion* is about its maintenance and nurture.

The distinction between these two dimensions may again be detected when Owen describes communion as 'God and the saints...walk[ing] together in a covenant of peace'.[2] In union with Christ the believer has, objectively, peace with God (Rom. 5:1). The peace is just a fact, irrespective of whether it is being felt, enjoyed and acted upon at a given moment. But Owen here looks beyond that bare, forensic reality. He envisages this peace passing from the realm of objective fact into the realm of meaningful, day-to-day expression. It is *walked in*. It is appropriated. It is experienced. It comes to life in an intimate, interactive relationship between God and the believer. That is what constitutes communion.

At certain points Owen's sober exposition of communion gives way to what he calls 'directions.' These are passionate exhortations to his readers, and they further demonstrate that communion is not simply a given. It is rather a practice in which the Christian must engage. In the directions on *communion with the Father*, the stress is on meditation: Owen uses the language of 'eye[ing]' the Father, 'look[ing] on him', entertaining a particular 'notion' of him; he says it is 'in the multitude of their *thoughts* [that] the comforts of

---

2. Ibid., 2:9.

God their Father refresh [believers'] souls.'[3] The directions on *communion with the Spirit* emphasise doxology: Owen speaks of 'returning praise, and thanks, and honour, and glory, and blessing to him'.[4] The material on *communion with the Son* (while lacking the actual term, 'directions') enjoins believers to relish Christ: Owen describes how 'the excellency of his person [and] his all-conquering desirableness...ravish their hearts, fill their affections, and possess their souls.'[5] Such meditation, doxology and relish are not facts intrinsic to the believer's relationship with God. They are activities which the believer must deliberately choose in order to develop that relationship.

The Biblical Data

But is communion with God, defined in this way, a biblical theme? Do the Scriptures look beyond that fixed *union* (with Christ) which is the constant, unchanging possession of every believer? Do they point also to a dynamic engagement with God, marked by intimacy and fervour? We must give an affirmative answer. The New Testament employs a range of terms, metaphors and even prepositions to express this reality. We shall briefly survey some of this biblical material. It will provide a useful basis for our subsequent Trinitarian reflections.

Participation

The obvious starting point is the New Testament's use of the word κοινωνία (*koinonia*). 'Participation' is the term's basic meaning, and it admits of a range of applications. In some cases, two human parties are in view, and there

---

3. Ibid., 2:32, 39 (italics mine).
4. Ibid., 2:271.
5. Ibid., 2:139.

is a specific entity in which they mutually participate. In Philippians 1:5, for example, Paul and the Philippian church mutually participate in the apostle's gospel ministry. In at least one case, a believer and a divine person are the two parties in view, and again there is a specific entity in which they mutually participate: it is mutual participation in *suffering* (Phil. 3:10).

However, a handful of texts employ the term when believers and divine persons are the parties in view and *no separate entity is mentioned* (1 Cor. 1:9; 2 Cor. 13:14; Phil. 2:1; 1 John 1:3). The two parties simply participate in each other! It suggests an involved relationship between God and the believer. It suggests a bond that is not merely 'on paper' but is actively entered into and enjoyed. It suggests communion.

Knowledge

Next, there is the γνῶσις (*gnosis*) word group. The nouns γνῶσις (*gnosis*) and ἐπίγνωσις (*epignosis*) essentially both mean 'knowledge'; the verb γινώσκω (*ginosko*), 'I know'. Often when these words are used in the New Testament, it is the knowledge of abstract information that is in view. Sometimes, however, it is the knowledge of a person. In such cases it is a much less cerebral phenomenon: it is not a set of data *about the person* that is known; it is the person him or herself. The apex of this interpersonal type of knowledge is sexual union between a husband and wife — the significance of γινώσκω (*ginosko*) in Matthew 1:25 and Luke 1:34. But even when the New Testament occurrences do not quite mean that, the suggestion of intimate relationship is never shaken off entirely. It is in that light that we must approach the numerous texts which speak of believers *knowing* divine persons (John 17:3; Eph. 1:17; 3:19; 4:13; Phil. 3:8, 10; Col. 1:10; 2 Pet. 3:18; 1 John 2:13-14; 4:7).

By writing in this way, the biblical authors were taking a risk. Among their readers were former pagans only too familiar with the concept of divine-human sexual relationships.[6] References to Christians *knowing* God were thus vulnerable to abhorrent misinterpretations. The substitution of an alternative, blander word might not have conveyed much relational intimacy, but would have at least distanced Christian piety from pagan perversions. That is the route one might expect those New Testament writers to have taken. It is a measure of how important it was to convey relational intimacy that, instead, they persisted with such hazardous vocabulary. They were determined to inculcate in the early disciples the necessity of communing with God. Nothing, not even the avoidance of gross miscomprehension, would make those authors settle for a Christianity that was merely static benefits received through union with Christ. The life of faith must rise higher than that. There must be more. There must be a living, vibrant relationship.[7]

Indwelling

A third group of communion texts is bound together conceptually rather than lexically. It comprises texts which speak of a divine *indwelling* experienced by the believer.

---

6. For instance, Gordon Fee refers to a 'story narrated in Josephus about the lady Paulina, who "after supper" at the temple had nightlong sex with Mundus, thinking he was the god Anubis' (Gordon D. Fee, *The First Epistle to the Corinthians* [Grand Rapids, Michigan: William B. Eerdmans Publishing Company, 1987], 455).

7. Owen recognises the relational significance of 'knowledge' texts in the New Testament when he cites 1 John 2:4 ('Whoever says "I know him" but does not keep his commandments is a liar') and then offers as his own paraphrase: 'Whoever says "I have communion with him"....' (Owen, *Works*, 2:39).

In the latter part of Ephesians 3, Paul tells the Ephesian believers some of the concerns which shape his prayers for them. It is important to understand that from the outset of the epistle he has been emphatic about their union with Christ. It has underpinned all the theology of Ephesians 1:3–3:13. Remarkably, however, he now tells them that a great concern in his prayers is 'that Christ may dwell in your hearts' (Eph. 3:17)! How can these Ephesian men and women have been united to Christ since conversion, and yet still be in need of Christ indwelling them?

There is a section in Calvin's *Institutes* which helps to illuminate Paul's logic. Calvin writes in the most robust terms of the believer's union with Christ:

> Since Christ has been communicated to you with all his benefits, so that all which is his is made yours, you become a member of him, and hence one with him. His righteousness covers your sins — his salvation extinguishes your condemnation; he interposes with his worthiness, and so prevents your unworthiness from coming into the view of God. Thus it truly is. It will never do to separate Christ from us, nor us from him; but we must, with both hands, keep firm hold of that alliance by which he has riveted us to himself.[8]

It sounds as though Calvin is describing such a bond with Christ as leaves no room for anything further. Surely, we can experience no more of Christ once he has 'riveted us to himself' — that must be the Omega Point! However, Calvin then adds a telling sentence: '[Christ] not only unites us to himself by an undivided bond of fellowship, *but by a wondrous communion brings us daily into closer*

---

8. John Calvin, *Institutes of the Christian Religion*, trans. Henry Beveridge (Grand Rapids, Michigan: Associated Publishers and Authors Inc., undated), 3.2.24.

connection, until he becomes altogether one with us.'[9] Even for those joined so profoundly to Christ at conversion, there is the possibility of a 'daily…closer connection'! That is the reason Paul can pray for long-standing Christian people to be indwelt by Christ. He is not denying the union that already exists: after all, it is only 'in him' that we can possibly 'have redemption through his blood, the forgiveness of our trespasses' (Eph. 1:7). Rather, Paul is praying that they will experience what Calvin calls 'wondrous communion.'

The same idea seems to be present in John 14:23, where Jesus describes the indwelling in the striking language of *making a home*. Importantly, he says that this divine homemaking occurs whenever 'anyone loves me [and] keep[s] my word'; it is triggered by the Christian's love and obedience. It is clear within the New Testament that while faith necessarily exists from the inception of the Christian life, moral virtues like love and obedience emerge subsequently and gradually. If the indwelling of John 14:23 is triggered by this gradually emerging love and obedience, it cannot be that initial divine entrance into an individual's life that constitutes the person a Christian. Jesus must have in mind the same thing that Paul does in Ephesians 3. It is in a deepening experience of communion that this indwelling consists.

In a similar vein are those texts which use temple language to refer to the believer. The outstanding text of this kind is 1 Corinthians 6:19.[10] It is evident, particularly in the Book of Psalms, that the divine indwelling in the Jerusalem temple

---

9. Ibid., 3.2.24 (italics mine).

10. Although Paul says specifically that 'your body is a temple', he clearly does not mean that the divine indwelling is *purely* a bodily reality. It is the believer's *person* that is the object of the indwelling. Paul simply wants to stress to his Corinthian readers, with their low view of the material realm, that the body is truly part of that indwelt person.

during the old covenant was oriented towards communion. In Psalm 42 the writer 'thirsts for God' and asks, 'when shall I come and appear before God?' (verse 2). What sort of thirst-quenching appearance before God does he have in mind? It soon becomes clear: 'These things I remember, as I pour out my soul: how I would go with the throng and lead them in procession to *the house of God*' (verse 4, italics mine). The temple is presented here as the locus of communion. Psalm 27:4 is even more explicit: 'One thing I ask of the LORD, this is what I seek: that I may dwell in the house of the LORD all the days of my life, to gaze upon the beauty of the LORD and to seek him in his temple.'[11] In the light of this Old Testament material, it is reasonable to infer that when the New Testament describes the Christian as a temple, there is likewise an emphasis on communion. The believer experiences a relational enjoyment of the indwelling God.

---

11. We must beware an overly functional conception of the old covenant temple, as though it were merely a mechanism for managing Israel's sins by means of animal sacrifices. The Old Testament consistently views the site in *residential* terms: it is a house, not an abattoir! Douglas Stuart (albeit referring to the temple's predecessor, the tabernacle) captures this well: 'The tabernacle represented Yahweh's house among the Israelites … He himself was symbolically represented as dwelling in the "back room" of his house by means of the ark. In the tabernacle's "front room" were several pieces of furniture, the sorts of things that represented the furniture of a home, though on a grander scale. The first of these pieces of household-style furniture to be described [in Exodus 25] is the table. It was primarily for food — a dining table of sorts, symbolising the fact that Yahweh really did live among his people and inhabit his house in much the same way that they inhabited theirs' (Douglas K. Stuart, *The New American Commentary*, vol. 2, *Exodus* [Nashville, Tennessee: B&H Publishing Group, 2006], 572). Consequently, the more comprehending Israelites did not go to the temple simply as guilty sinners in search of atonement. They went to it, too, as Yahweh's guests, humbly accepting the invitation to enjoy his hospitality and spend time in his presence.

Proximity

There is a fourth class of communion texts not dissimilar to the one just considered. In this case, however, the perspective is altered slightly. If the *indwelling* passages present God as being close to the believer, these passages present the believer as being close to God. *Proximity* is the term I have chosen to capture the idea.

The New Testament uses two verbs to convey the idea of entering God's presence: one is ἐγγίζω (*eggizo*) (Heb. 7:19; James 4:8); the other, προσέρχομαι (*proserchomai*) (Heb. 4:16; 7:25; 10:22; 11:6; 1 Pet. 2:4). Interestingly, like γινώσκω (*ginosko*), προσέρχομαι (*proserchomai*) can have a sexual meaning: in the Septuagint it is used of Isaiah's 'approach' to his wife which resulted in the conception of their son (Isa. 8:3). As we remarked with the other sexual term, the New Testament clearly is not making a blasphemous suggestion about the Christian's relationship with the true God. But at the same time the writer of Hebrews, who was familiar with Isaiah 8,[12] may have wanted *some* of the intimacy of the prophet's usage to spill over into his own.

The reality of the believer dwelling close to God is in fact the theme of some of the New Testament's grandest declarations. 1 Peter 3:18 summarises the whole of redemption in terms of people being brought to God. Ephesians 2:18 has a similarly epic quality when it states with reference to God: 'we ... have access'![13] Declarations like these portray the Christian life as a markedly Godward life, a life of communion.

Ingestion

A fifth group of communion texts is very small but significant enough to merit inclusion in our survey. It centres upon

---

12. Hebrews 2:13 cites Isaiah 8:18.
13. Ephesians 3:12 uses the same language.

the theme of *ingestion*. These texts describe the believer eating and drinking God. D.A. Carson explains how the trope works:

> We must appropriate him into our inmost being. Indeed ... we are more familiar with this...metaphor than we may realise: we devour books, drink in lectures, swallow stories, ruminate on ideas, chew over a matter ... Doting grandparents declare they could eat up their grandchildren.[14]

The number of idioms Carson is able to cite indicates the ingestion metaphor has an intrinsic intelligibility. It conveys, almost axiomatically, the idea of *intense engagement with a person or thing*. But the first Christians were able to view the metaphor through the additional lens of their Old Testament knowledge. That only reinforced its meaning. In Psalm 63:5, for example, David anticipates bouts of nocturnal meditation on God (verse 6) and predicts that his soul 'will be satisfied as with fat and rich food'. Similarly, in Psalm 34:8 he extols Yahweh's goodness as something not merely to be heard of or acknowledged, but actually *tasted*.

When, therefore, the original readers of the New Testament documents encountered ingestion statements like those in 1 Corinthians 12:13 and John 7:37 (in both of which the focus is on drinking), or the repeated one in John 6 (verses 51, 53-58; the focus is on both drinking and eating), they knew exactly what was meant. Paul and Jesus were describing the same kind of intense engagement with God that had so captivated David centuries earlier. Like him, they found in the activities of eating and drinking a fine depiction of that earnest communion which appropriates God into the depths of one's soul.

---

14. D.A. Carson, *The Gospel According to St John* (Leicester: Apollos, 1991), 279.

Walking

Finally, there is another metaphorical description of communion which occurs once in the New Testament: *walking* with God (Rev. 3:4). We have already noted Owen's usage of this evocative picture. Like the concept of ingesting God, the concept of walking with him is rooted in the Old Testament, particularly the remarkable tribute to Enoch which occurs twice in Genesis 5: 'Enoch walked with God' (verses 22, 24).[15] According to Gordon Wenham, it is the ardent devotional bent of the man's life which the writer wished to express: 'The phrase suggests a special intimacy with God.'[16]

Given the extent to which the last book of the Bible draws on the language and imagery of the first,[17] it seems natural to connect the walking in Revelation 3:4 with the walking of Enoch (and, possibly, that of Adam and Eve; see fn. 15). The reference occurs within a promise to the faithful members of the church in Sardis. They will walk with God 'in white'. Given that in the following verse *wearing white garments* is the privilege of 'the one who conquers,' the passage probably has an eschatological orientation. This walking with God belongs to the coming age. But, chronological considerations aside, it is the *meaning* of the walking that is important for

---

15. The roots of this imagery may reach even further back than Genesis 5. On the day that Adam ate the prohibited fruit, God walked 'in the garden in the cool of the day' (Gen. 3:8). It may reasonably be inferred (though not proved) that he did this regularly, and that, prior to this day, it had been Adam and Eve's practice to walk with him.

16. Gordon J. Wenham, *Word Biblical Commentary*, vol. 1, *Genesis 1-15* (Waco, Texas: Word Books, 1987), 127.

17. Examples include: paradise (Rev. 2:7), the rainbow (4:3), the serpent (20:2), heaven and earth (21:1), the tree of life (22:2), and the frequent recurrence of the number seven.

our purposes. It conjures the image of two persons enjoying one another's company as they move along together arm-in-arm, each striding out in unison with the other. It signifies the believers of Sardis, like Enoch, revelling in rich communion with God.

An Incontrovertible Case

This survey is not exhaustive. It is sufficient, however, to present an incontrovertible case. Through the language and imagery of *participation, knowledge, indwelling, proximity, ingestion* and *walking,* the New Testament indicates there is a dimension of dynamic communion to the believer's relationship with God. By itself the concept of *union* is inadequate to accommodate this substantial vein of biblical material. The additional concept of *communion with God* is necessary.

Communion with God, therefore, is not a Puritan invention. It was not some over-experiential, anti-intellectual movement within church history that foisted the idea on Christianity. And nor does it compromise the apostolic doctrine that the humblest believer is fully and irreversibly united to Christ in the moment of regeneration. Rather, union and communion are complementary, equally glorious dimensions of New Testament Christianity.

But with whom *exactly* is the believer's communion?

CHAPTER TWO

Communion and the Divine Persons

At one level the answer to the previous chapter's closing question is simple. With whom is the believer's communion? It is with *God*, of course! When we start to consider the profundities of God's being, however, the inadequacy of that answer is quickly exposed. For the most fundamental truth about the God of the Bible — the truth affirmed at the initiation of every Christian life (Matt. 28:19) — is that he exists as three persons. He is Father, Son, and Holy Spirit.[1] This throws our question into sharp relief. It

---

1. The doctrine of the Trinity is here simply presupposed; an abundance of literature may be consulted for the supporting evidence and arguments. While its stripped-down approach does not meet with universal approval, B.B. Warfield's three-point statement of the doctrine remains, in my view, compelling: 'We may content ourselves with simply observing that to the New Testament there is but one only living and true God; but that to it Jesus Christ and the Holy Spirit are each God in the fullest sense of the term; and yet Father, Son and Spirit stand over against each other as I, and Thou, and He. In this composite fact the New Testament gives us the doctrine of the Trinity ... When we have said these three things, then — that there is but one God, that the Father and the Son and the Spirit is each God, that the

is not a vapid query. It is not a glaring insult to the reader's intelligence. No, the triune nature of God necessitates clarity on this point: with whom *exactly* is the believer's communion?

John Owen's answer is emphatic: 'The saints have distinct communion with the Father, and the Son, and the Holy Spirit (that is, distinctly with the Father, and distinctly with the Son, and distinctly with the Holy Spirit)'.[2] The parenthesis in that sentence may appear superfluous. It reveals, however, the Puritan's determination to establish this point about *distinctness of communion*. It is not merely that Christians commune with a God who happens to exist, it later emerges, as distinct persons. Rather, their communion is wholly conditioned by that reality. It adopts a triadic shape corresponding to the triadic shape of God. Owen risks tautology here in order to impress this indelibly on his readers' minds. Indeed, it is notable that, whenever he subsequently restates the concept, he does so in almost unvarying terms (the substitution of 'severally' for 'distinctly' being a rare deviation at one point).[3] Literary flair is not Owen's priority; driving home his paradigm of tri-personal communion *is*!

Returning to the Biblical Data

Again, then, we must go to the Scriptures. We have established in the previous chapter that Owen is thoroughly

---

Father and the Son and the Spirit is each a distinct person — we have enunciated the doctrine of the Trinity in its completeness' (B.B. Warfield, 'The Biblical Doctrine of the Trinity,' in *Biblical and Theological Studies*, ed. Samuel G. Craig [Philadelphia, Pennsylvania: Presbyterian and Reformed, 1968], 35-36).

2. John Owen, *Of Communion with God the Father, Son, and Holy Ghost, Each Person Distinctly, in Love, Grace, and Consolation* (1657), in *The Works of John Owen*, ed. William H. Goold (Edinburgh: Banner of Truth, 2004), 2:9.

3. Ibid., 2:10.

biblical in his distinction between the believer's union and the believer's communion. Is he also biblical in these further distinctions *within* the believer's communion — these Trinitarian distinctions? Again, we may give an affirmative answer. If we revisit our earlier survey with this new question in mind, we discover that our results were in fact richly Trinitarian. Admittedly, it is not the case that all six New Testament expressions of communion that we identified — *participation, knowledge, indwelling, proximity, ingestion* and *walking* — are explicitly connected with all three divine persons. It certainly is the case, however, that when the six expressions are taken together, all three persons are amply represented. The following, brief summary makes that clear.

1. The believer's *participation* is in the Spirit (2 Cor. 13:14; Phil. 2:1), in the Son (1 Cor. 1:9;) and, according to 1 John 1:3, in the Son and the Father.

2. Sometimes the object of the believer's *knowledge* is said to be the Father (Eph. 1:17; Col. 1:10; 1 John 2:13; 4:7), sometimes the Son (Eph. 3:19; 4:13; Phil. 3:8, 10; 2 Pet. 3:18) and, in John 17:3, the Father and the Son.

3. The *indwelling* is connected in one place with the Spirit (1 Cor. 6:19),[4] in another place with the Son (Eph. 3:17) and, in John 14:23, with the Son and the Father.

4. The state of *proximity* into which the believer has been brought is with reference to the Father (Eph. 2:18; Heb. 7:19, 25; 10:22; 11:6; James 4:8; 1 Pet. 3:18), with

---

4. The reader is reminded that the indwelling in view here is that which may be designated *communion* (the use of temple language, we established, permits such an inference). There are other texts which speak of the Spirit's indwelling but where the emphasis is not on the believer's communion with him.

reference to the Son (1 Pet. 2:4) and, according to Hebrews 4:16, with reference to the Father and the Son.[5]

5. The metaphor of *ingestion* is applied to the believer's relations with the Spirit (1 Cor. 12:13; John 7:37) and to the believer's relations with the Son (John 6:51, 53-58).

6. Finally, it is the Son with whom the believer is said to *walk* (Rev. 3:4).

Clearly, then, the believer's communion is with all three divine persons. Owen's Trinitarian boldness in the realm of Christian devotion is warranted by the New Testament's Trinitarian boldness in that realm. The inspired Scriptures do not show more reserve than the seventeenth-century theologian.

If anything, in fact, they show even less reserve. For there is another angle from which we may approach the New Testament material we have already amassed. The results yielded by this shift of perspective are striking.

The Distinction Between *Object* and *Facilitator* of Communion

Several of our communion texts mention more than one divine person. In a number of these texts the point is simply that we commune with each of the persons mentioned. In others, however, there is a subtle distinction in the ways that the divine persons are involved: the communion is only with one (or possibly two) of the persons mentioned. Whichever other persons are mentioned serve as facilitators of that communion. They make it possible.

---

5. It is actually 'the throne of grace' to which the believer 'draws near' in this verse, but in the theology of Hebrews that is a throne on which the Father sits and where the Son is at 'the right hand' (1:3, 13; 8:1; 10:12; 12:2). In 4:16 the Son at the right hand is certainly in view; the seated Father is implied.

An example of this is Ephesians 2:18: 'For through [Christ] we...have access in one Spirit to the Father.' Here, the communion is actually with the Father: he is the person being accessed by the believer. That communion is facilitated, however, by Christ (probably a reference to his atoning work on the cross; cf. verse 16) and by the Spirit (probably a reference to his assuring ministry in the heart; cf. Rom. 8:15-16). Their operations are indispensable: without Christ, guilt would preclude communion with the Father; without the Spirit, fear would stifle it. But the communion is not actually with either of those persons. In this text the Father is in the foreground as the person with whom the believer is engaging; the Son and Spirit are in the background effecting that engagement.

We are now ready to approach our texts from the different 'angle' previously mentioned. Our earlier question was, 'Which divine persons may be the object of the believer's communion?' 'All of them' was the answer! An alternative question presents itself: 'Which divine persons may facilitate the believer's communion with another divine person?' We have established that in Ephesians 2:18 the Son and the Spirit facilitate the believer's communion with the Father. That arrangement may appear unsurprising. We might assume, indeed, that it is normative. However, our New Testament data yields some intriguing insights.

All Three Persons Facilitate Communion

We discover in the first place that to the Father, too, the facilitating role may be attributed. In John 6 Jesus' use of ingestion imagery is extensive and varied. At points the flesh and blood motif dominates. At other points manna typology is to the fore. In that latter connection he makes this statement: 'Truly, truly, I say to you, it was not Moses who gave you the bread from heaven, but my Father gives you the true bread from heaven' (John 6:32). By 'the true bread from heaven' he is referring, of course, to himself. In this text, then, communion is with the Son (feeding on the bread from heaven), and it is brought about by the Father (giving the bread from heaven). The question of whether the Father's bread-giving refers here to his sending of the Son in the incarnation, or to his regenerating activity in the life of a sinner, is probably foreign to the concerns of the text.[6] Either way, the result is a communion with the Son which has been facilitated by the Father.

The same arrangement is explicit in 1 Corinthians 1:9: 'God is faithful, by whom you were called into the fellowship of his Son.' In most New Testament instances, the 'call' of the Father is not a mere invitation but an irresistible summons. He calls 'according to his purpose' (Rom. 8:28). This call can no more be refused than God's purpose can be frustrated. In the language of Reformed soteriology, it is 'effectual'. It unfailingly makes something happen. In this text it is communion with the Son that the call makes happen. If that communion-creating call issues from the Father, then to the Father is attributed a communion-creating role.

But our data yields other unexpected configurations. The Father and Son do not merely facilitate each other's communion with the believer; they also perform that role in relation to the Spirit's communion with the believer.

In 2 Corinthians 13:14 Paul's prayer for his readers is that 'The grace of the Lord Jesus Christ and the love of God and the fellowship of the Holy Spirit be with you all.'[7] Elsewhere

---

6. The soteriological distinction in later theology between the *historia salutis* and the *ordo salutis*, while immensely helpful, cannot neatly be brought to bear on every biblical text which relates to salvation.

7. Philippians 2:1 appears to be a close parallel to this text: 'If

in Paul's writing, the Son's grace and the Father's love are not static attributes. They are intimately associated with the accomplishment of redemption. In 2 Corinthians 8:9 Christ's grace is his becoming 'poor, so that you by his poverty might become rich.' In Romans 5:8 God's love comes into its own at the cross. It is likely that these associations are present in 2 Corinthians 13:14. Paul is referring specifically to the self-giving grace of the Son and the Son-giving love of the Father. There appears, then, to be a redemptive 'flow' to the text: the work of the Son and the Father in redemptive history leads to the believer's present communion with the Spirit. That communion is the terminus of a redemption grounded in the events of incarnation and atonement. As the Son graciously engaged in his saving activity, and the Father lovingly engaged in his, they were securing for the believer this intimate fellowship with the Spirit.[8]

there is any encouragement in Christ, any comfort from love, any participation in the Spirit ...' 'In light of their linguistic similarities to 2 Cor 13:13 (14) ... these three clauses very likely also reflect an intentional Trinitarian substructure' (Gordon D. Fee, *Paul's Letter to the Philippians* [Grand Rapids, Michigan: William B. Eerdmans Publishing Company, 1995], 179).

8. My use of this text involves the grammatical assumption that ἡ κοινωνία τοῦ ἁγίου πνεύματος (*he koinonia tou hagiou pneumatos*) is an objective genitive. If it were a subjective genitive, then the reference would be to a fellowship *between human beings* that is effected by the Spirit. That seems unlikely. As noted in the previous chapter, when κοινωνία (*koinonia*) has two human parties in view there is normally an indication of a specific 'entity' in which they mutually participate. John alone refers to horizontal fellowship without mentioning any such entity (1 John 1:3, 7). If 2 Corinthians 13:14 contains such a reference, it is unparalleled within the Pauline corpus. When Paul writes about κοινωνία (*koinonia*) without identifying *that which is participated in*, believers and divine persons are the parties in view. It seems best to assume that meaning here.

One further text which deserves attention is 1 Corinthians 12:13. At several points in 1 Corinthians Paul tackles an elitism which seems to have infected some of his readers.[9] A section of the Corinthian church is intoxicated with its own superiority. This is the problem Paul is addressing in 1 Corinthians 12:13. His argument here is that irrespective of external, superficial distinctions between them, the Corinthian believers were 'all made to drink of one Spirit.' Like John 6 this is a passage where the believer's deep appropriation of a divine person is expressed in terms of *ingestion*. Here, however, the Spirit rather than the Son is the person ingested. And one aspect of Paul's statement can easily be missed: the verb (ἐποτίσθημεν, *epotisthemen*) is in the passive voice. The Corinthian believers have not simply drunk of the Spirit; they have *been made to* drink of him.[10] The undisclosed subject of the verb — the one who effects the drinking — is presumably one (or possibly both) of the other divine persons. Like 2 Corinthians 13:14, this text describes a communion with the Spirit that is made possible by the Father and/or the Son. The Spirit is its object; they are its facilitators.[11]

---

9. Examples of Paul doing this may be found in 4:6-7, 8:1-2 and 11:22.

10. The passive of ποτίζω (*potizo*) is not easily translated into English. The ESV's translation, adopted here, could convey a sense of coercion which is entirely lacking in the Greek. 'Given … to drink' (NIV) is something of an over-translation, but at least avoids that other connotation.

11. The verse as a whole seems to make the drinking of the Spirit a consequence of baptism in the Spirit. On the basis that the Son is the one who baptises believers with the Spirit (Luke 3:16), he may be the obvious person to identify as *facilitator* here. But the evidence is not strong enough to rule out decisively a reference to the Father's facilitating activity.

The Spirit as a Case Study

The significance of all this may appear more clearly if we briefly narrow our focus to a single divine person. We shall choose the Spirit. Consider the following:

- According to Romans 8:15-16 the Spirit exercises an *assuring* ministry within the believer: he 'bears witness with our spirit that we are children of God'. This enables the believer to commune with the Father: 'by [him] we cry "Abba! Father!"'

- According to Ephesians 1:17 the Spirit exercises an *enlightening* ministry within the believer: he is the Spirit 'of wisdom and of revelation'. This, too, enables the believer to commune with the Father: he is the Spirit 'of wisdom and of revelation in the knowledge of him'.

- According to Ephesians 3:16-17 the Spirit exercises a *sanctifying* ministry within the believer: his strengthening 'with power…in your inner being' would appear to have that moral sense. This enables the believer to commune with the Son: 'strengthened with power through his Spirit in your inner being so that Christ may dwell in your hearts'.

In these texts, then, an act of divine-human communion *arises out of* the Spirit's background activity, but it *culminates in* a different divine person. That is the direction of travel.

In other passages, however, the opposite is the case. The Spirit is 'the blessing of Abraham,' released to the believer through the Son's accursed death (Gal. 3:13-14). He is the believer's thirst-quenching drink (1 Cor. 12:13; John 7:37). Believers are temples of the Holy Spirit (1 Cor. 6:19). In these texts the direction of travel is reversed. The Spirit is now at the other end of the act of communion: in the foreground; at the point where it culminates; at the interface between God and the believer. 'The Spirit is nothing other than God in his saving presence in communion with ... the human being.'[12]

Bold Devotional Trinitarianism

John Owen, as we saw, writes in bold terms. Discussing the believer's communion with the tri-personal God, he almost bludgeons the reader with those words 'distinct' and 'distinctly'! But Owen's boldness is matched — exceeded even — by the New Testament. We have discovered in this chapter that not only does the New Testament portray Christian communion as person-specific; it goes beyond that in two ways.

In the first place, it is not amenable to the idea that communion is with just one or two (more dominant and public-facing) divine persons. Instead, the believer engages directly with them all. When the language of divine-human intimacy (as surveyed in the previous chapter) is used, the Father or the Son or the Spirit can be primarily in view.

But nor, secondly, is the New Testament amenable to the idea that communion is effected by just one or two (less dominant, less public-facing) divine persons. All of them contribute behind the scenes to each other's divine-human relations.[13] That is remarkable. Christian devotion is so

---

12. Mark A. Seifrid, *The Second Letter to the Corinthians* (Nottingham: Apollos, 2014), 499. On this point of the Spirit as terminus or culmination — something which can cause unease in the conservative evangelical mind (see chapter seven) — an aside by Karl Barth is of interest. He refers to the thirteenth-century Italian bishop, Bonaventure, assigning 'principle to the Father, execution to the Son and *goal to the Spirit*' (Karl Barth, *Church Dogmatics*, ed. Thomas F. Torrance and Geoffrey W. Bromiley, trans. Geoffrey W. Bromiley [Edinburgh: T & T Clark, 1956], I/1: 373 [italics mine]).

13. A stimulating remark by Donald Macleod may be relevant

pervasively Trinitarian that it eludes any rigid, formulaic attempts to hierarchise the believer's three-way relationship.[14]

However, this devotional Trinitarian boldness needs to be subjected to further scrutiny. God, after all, is one. Is it

here: 'One may...ask...whether the persons of the Godhead do not seem to vie with one another for the privilege of serving. The gospels indicate not only a service performed by the Son for the Father but also a ministry...on the part of the Father for the Son' (Donald Macleod, *The Person of Christ* [Leicester: Inter-Varsity Press, 1998], 88). Macleod's reference to 'the gospels' shows that he has in mind, primarily, the *accomplishment* phase of redemption. It seems reasonable to expect, however, that this intra-Trinitarian competition(!), if real, would manifest itself also in the *application* phase of redemption. Perhaps it takes the form outlined in this chapter: the persons 'vying' to put each other in the foreground of communion; each selflessly desiring to facilitate the others' relationships with the believer.

14. It is in my opinion an unfortunate inconsistency in Owen that, despite his emphasis on communing distinctly and directly with all the persons, he does not always avoid the gravitational pull of rigid, hierarchising formulae. He refers at one point to Ephesians 2:18 as 'that heavenly directory' (*Works*, 2:269), as though it were the *locus classicus* and normative for Trinitarian communion. But as argued above, that text features communion with one person alone. Thus, by the logic of Owen's treatise as a whole, it cannot be made the paradigm of what tri-personal communion looks like. He recognises that in 2 Corinthians 13:14 '[communion with] the Spirit alone is mentioned' (*Works*, 2:11) despite the other two persons being involved; surely, the same is true with respect to the Father in Ephesians 2:18.

It is possible that Owen had a methodological bias toward finding a single biblical 'directory,' and this made Ephesians 2:18 disproportionately endearing to him. Finding that one, definitive text which encapsulates everything is always enticing for *any* theologian arguing for *any* point of doctrine. The Owen scholar, Brian Kay, wishes the Puritan had adopted more of a 'cumulative evidence' approach in his marshalling of biblical texts regarding Trinitarian communion (Brian Kay, *Trinitarian Spirituality: John Owen and the Doctrine of God in Western Devotion* [Milton Keynes: Paternoster, 2007], 121-22).

possible, therefore, for the divine persons to be so *distinctly* involved in Christian communion? And are there not texts in the New Testament in which God is approached in an *indistinct* way?

The first of those questions will be the main concern of part two of this book. To the second question, however, we must now turn.

CHAPTER THREE

Relating to the Three
as Both They and He

In chapter one we identified six New Testament descriptions of communion with God, and we probed these further in chapter two. These descriptions, of course, are impressionistic in their character. *Ingestion* and *walking*, to mention two, capture well the essence of communion. They tell us nothing, however, of how it works in practice. God is not literally eaten and drunk by the saints; nor does he literally accompany the believer on a stroll! A more prosaic account of Christian communion, then, would emphasise such activities as prayer, hearing God's word and partaking of the Lord's Supper. It is through these that *ingestion, walking, participation* and the rest take place.

When, in part three of this book, we come to the practical outworking of distinct communion, we shall focus particularly on the activity of prayer. But we have reached a point *now* at which certain New Testament references to prayer need to be considered. For prayer is sometimes mentioned in such a way that the distinctness of the divine persons does not seem to be relevant. These references appear to undermine the pervasive devotional Trinitarianism emphasised in the previous chapter.

Non-specific Texts About Prayer

An example is Romans 10:1. There, Paul shares with his readers his burden for the unbelieving Jews. He writes of his 'prayer to God for them...that they may be saved.' Nothing in the context enables us to identify 'God,' here, with one particular divine person. The same is true when Paul assures the Corinthians, 'We pray to God that you may not do wrong' (2 Cor. 13:7). To whom, then, is Paul offering these prayers?[1] Has he in these instances forgotten that the God of Christian communion is tri-personal?

It might appear as though I am creating an issue where there is none. Does it really matter if in a small selection of texts there are references to prayer which seem sub-Trinitarian? Before dismissing the matter as unimportant, however, we should note the words of an eighteenth-century Socinian named Paul Cardale. He baited the Trinitarians of his day with this remark: 'Had it been possible for St. Paul to entertain the doctrine of a Trinity, he would no doubt have directed his own prayers...to the Sacred Three, as is

---

1. 1 Corinthians 11:13 provides another example. Moreover, the phenomenon surfaces outside of Paul's writings. It may be seen in James 1:5 among other places.

Of course, there are texts about praying to 'God' in which it is made clear that the Father, specifically, is being addressed. In Acts 4:24, for instance, the Jerusalem church lifts its 'voices together to God'. This 'God' is then praised for what he has spoken 'by the Holy Spirit' (verse 25) and for his 'holy servant Jesus' (verse 27). 'God' is thus distinguished from the Spirit and the Son; the reference in this case must be to the Father. My concern in this chapter, however, is with those texts in which 'God' is addressed and in which it is not clear from the context that the Father is intended.

the common language of the present age.'[2] Clearly, then, the absence of hypostatic differentiation[3] in some texts about prayer does require attention. It has led at times to far-reaching (and disturbing) conclusions.

Being unable to adopt Cardale's Socinian approach, what are our options in respect of the non-specific texts? Let us begin with two contrasting possibilities. One approach to these texts applies very sharply to them the concept of personal distinctions in the Godhead. It assumes that prayers to 'God' in the New Testament are always prayers to one of the three persons, namely, the Father. This is an extrapolation from those biblical passages in which 'God' certainly does refer to the Father alone (see fn. 1). It is essentially the ancient hermeneutical principle of interpreting Scripture with Scripture: understanding the unclear references to 'God' in the light of the clear ones.

The other, opposite approach to these texts does not apply to them at all the concept of personal distinctions in the Godhead. It assumes that although God *is* tri-personal, that fact need not always be in view as the believer relates to him — and is not in view in the texts in question. God can be addressed as a single, undifferentiated being. Old covenant

---

2. Quoted in Michael A.G. Haykin, 'To Devote Ourselves to the Blessed Trinity,' in *One God in Three Persons: Unity of Essence, Distinction of Persons, Implications for Life*, ed. Bruce A. Ware and John Starke (Wheaton, Illinois: Crossway, 2015), 184. Haykin encountered Cardale's words in the work of another eighteenth-century Socinian, Joseph Priestley. It was in expounding Philippians 4:6 ('Let your requests be made known to God') that Cardale made the remark.

3. Though the term *hypostasis* has a complex back story — both etymologically and within the history of Trinitarian theology — in this book I assume its (fairly) standard modern definition, *person*. My use of the adjective 'hypostatic,' therefore, simply denotes *having to do with persons*.

believers, lacking the knowledge of divine tri-personality, prayed in that way.[4] New covenant believers, while possessing that knowledge, may still sometimes do so, too.

A Better Approach

Before feeling bound to decide between these two alternatives, we should consider a further option which veers to neither extreme. James Torrance offers an immensely penetrating insight when he writes:

> Christian worship is trinitarian in three main ways: We pray to the Father, through the Son, in the Spirit.... We pray to each of the three persons.... We glorify the one God, Father, Son and Holy Spirit'.[5]

---

4. I am aware some hold the position that Old Testament religion was in fact self-consciously Trinitarian. Paul Blackham, for instance, calls Moses 'that most brilliant and careful Trinitarian theologian' (Paul Blackham, 'The Trinity in the Hebrew Scriptures,' in *Trinitarian Soundings in Systematic Theology*, ed. Paul Louis Metzger [London: T & T Clark, 2006], 46). The main argument of Blackham and others is that the first Christians could not have accepted so readily the deity of Jesus unless they already possessed from their Scriptures a Trinitarian consciousness. But in my view this takes insufficient account of the overwhelming manifestation of divinity they encountered in Jesus. Swept along by such force of evidence, they could not *but* incorporate hypostatic plurality into their conception of God; they did not require any prior categories to help them. As Richard Bauckham puts it, 'The decisive step of including Jesus in the unique identity of God was...taken simply for its own sake and *de novo*' (Richard Bauckham, *Jesus and the God of Israel: God Crucified and Other Studies on the New Testament's Christology of Divine Identity* [Milton Keynes: Paternoster, 2008], 20).

5. James B. Torrance, *Worship, Community and the Triune God of Grace* (Downers Grove, Illinois: Inter-Varsity Press, 1996), 36.

These are not mutually exclusive devotional paths. Torrance is not proposing the acceptance of one and rejection of the others. Rather, the believer at different points prays in all three of these ways.

And the third type of prayer in the quote is relevant to the New Testament texts we are presently considering: texts in which intercessions are addressed simply to 'God'. In Torrance's terms they are prayers to 'the one God, Father, Son and Holy Spirit.' This understanding of them avoids, on the one hand, the rather arbitrary singling out of the Father where nothing in the immediate context encourages it. And it avoids, on the other hand, importing into these texts a sub-hypostatic notion of God. For, while disagreeing with Paul Blackham on the pace of Scripture's revelation of the Trinity (see fn. 4), I heartily endorse his insistence that 'God is nothing other than these Three Persons.'[6] There is no essence of God *prior to* or *separate from* the persons — and permitting an approach to God in which Father, Son and Spirit are out of the picture. We must not think that God in his threeness is *persons*, while God in his oneness is not. His oneness is not a substance or god-ness in which the persons share, and which can alternate with the persons as the object of the worshipper's attention. No, God's oneness *is* the persons; the persons so perfectly and entirely dwelling within each other that they are one. Gregory Nazianzen

---

6. Blackham, op. cit., 44. In this connection Blackham rightly takes issue with theologians whose 'doctrine of God... begins with a definition of a single divine essence before later (and usually much more briefly) dealing with the three divine persons' (ibid., 35). Nick Needham has made similar criticisms of that approach, describing it as 'a mysticism of the divine essence' (Nick Needham, 'The *Filioque* Clause: East or West?,' *Scottish Bulletin of Evangelical Theology* 15 [1997], 160).

expressed the matter succinctly: 'When I say God, I mean Father, Son, and Holy Spirit.'[7]

It is my contention that when New Testament writers said 'God,' they meant that, too. Consequently, when their prayers were to 'God,' they *were* engaging in Trinitarian communion, but they were on those occasions communing with God in the *unity* of his tri-personal existence rather than in the *plurality* of his tri-personal existence. And that must remain a valid devotional possibility. As Torrance makes clear in the words I quoted, it is not the *only* devotional possibility; nor is it the devotional possibility with which this book is primarily concerned. (The distinct communion of this book is to be identified, of course, with Torrance's second type of Trinitarian worship — 'We pray to each of the three persons.') But its validity ought to be acknowledged, nevertheless.

Gregory Nazianzen famously rhapsodised about an oscillation within his own communion with God:

> This I give you to share, and to defend all your life, the One Godhead and power, found in the Three in Unity, and comprising the Three separately ... No sooner do I conceive of the One than I am illumined by the Splendour of the Three; no sooner do I distinguish Them than I am carried back to the One. When I think of any One of the Three I think of Him as the Whole, and my eyes are filled ... When

---

7. Gregory Nazianzen, *Orations* 38.8, in *The Nicene and Post-Nicene Fathers*, vol. 7, ed. Philip Schaff and Henry Wace (Grand Rapids, Michigan: Wm. B. Eerdmans Publishing Company, 1978), 347. Cf. B.B. Warfield, who describes God's oneness as 'a unity of interpenetration' — that is, a unity resulting from the consummate co-inherence of three persons (B.B. Warfield, 'The Biblical Doctrine of the Trinity,' in *Biblical and Theological Studies*, ed. Samuel G. Craig [Philadelphia, Pennsylvania: Presbyterian and Reformed, 1968], 38).

I contemplate the Three together, I see but one torch, and cannot divide or measure out the Undivided Light.[8]

The desire, then, to recover and emphasise the concept of distinct communion does not mean the abandonment of other ways of relating to the triune God. There is a place for the believer to 'contemplate the Three together [and] see but one torch'. Even the champion of distinct communion, Owen himself, gave expression to that other side of the devotional oscillation. Kelly Kapic observes that:

> Owen's stress on distinction allows him to freely use the third-person plural pronoun "they"... when referring to the Father, Son, and Spirit. However, at other times Owen may refer to the three by employing the third-person singular pronoun "he."[9]

It is proper for the Christian to relate to the three in terms of *he-ness* as well as in terms of *they-ness*.

Using the Psalms

Relating to the three in singular language is necessary when using the biblical psalms. Different sections of the Christian church may not use the psalms to the same extent in their engagement with God, but all use them to some degree. Yet, unlike a modern hymnbook, the Book of Psalms does not comprise items which address the Father, items which address the Son and items which address the Spirit. *God* — designated by different names and titles — is the sole addressee.

---

8. Gregory Nazianzen, *Orations* 40.41, ibid., 375.

9. Kelly M. Kapic, *Communion with God: The Divine and the Human in the Theology of John Owen* (Grand Rapids, Michigan: Baker Academic, 2007), 159.

I mentioned earlier the absence of a Trinitarian consciousness in the old covenant period. It was natural, therefore, for the psalmists straightforwardly to address their compositions to *God*; they conceived of him in unipersonal terms. How, then, should *we think* as we approach God with these ancient lyrics on our lips? Do they permit only a unipersonal form of communion with God?

It is, of course, a cardinal principle of biblical hermeneutics that the understanding of the original author must always be taken seriously. However, that is not the only principle that should dictate our Christian usage of the psalms. Two other factors are also relevant.

First, it is right to shine new covenant light on old covenant Scriptures. We do not have to shrink our theological understanding to that of the psalmists and sing their material entertaining exactly the same ideas which they entertained. If we now know God to be three persons, we may flood the psalmists' references to him with that additional knowledge. This does not involve contradicting or correcting the psalms, for nowhere do they refute hypostatic plurality; it simply lies beyond their purview. Everything they say about God remains forever true but is *expanded and given texture* by our knowledge of the Trinity.

Secondly, it is only when they are used with a Trinitarian consciousness that the psalms as a phenomenon are explainable. Within their own theological milieu, they harbour a lurking awkwardness. They assume a God who is intensely relational — the intimacy of their engagement with him is the psalms' chief characteristic.[10] But only as

---

10. Owen seems unduly reluctant to recognise this. He writes: 'Communion and fellowship with God is not in express terms mentioned in the Old Testament ... Though [Old Testament saints] had communion with God, yet they had not...boldness and confidence in that communion' (John Owen, *Of Communion with*

a plurality of persons *can* God truly be relational. A God whose being is eternally and essentially undifferentiated might be a fitting object of obedience and submission, but not communion. 'A unipersonal god would not have within

---

God the Father, Son, and Holy Ghost, Each Person Distinctly, in Love, Grace, and Consolation [1657], in *The Works of John Owen*, ed. William H. Goold [Edinburgh: Banner of Truth, 2004], 2:6). He bases this on the theological consideration that Christ had not yet entered heaven to make bold communion possible. But this is problematic for a couple of reasons.

First, there is not a tight chronological relationship between the *history* of redemption and the *application* of redemption; the latter can race ahead of the former. Put otherwise, in the gradual unfolding of salvation, benefits can be subjectively experienced which have not yet been objectively secured. Calvin recognises this when he describes 'the Fathers under the Law' having benefits 'transferred to them from another source…transferred to the Law from the Gospel' (John Calvin, *Calvin's Commentaries*, vol. 10, *Jeremiah 20-47*, trans. and ed. John Owen [Grand Rapids, Michigan: Baker Books, 2003], 131).

Indeed, without this 'transfer' the old covenant saints would not even have experienced the shadowy form of communion which Owen permits them; they would have experienced *no communion* — for how can there be any fellowship with God for sinners apart from what Christ secured? And if what Christ secured *was* transferred to them, then why should they not have experienced bold, full-orbed communion? Interestingly, Owen includes among the divine 'acts and workings…which are common to both [old covenant and new covenant] states of the church' the 'effectual dispensation of sanctifying grace towards the elect of God' (John Owen, *A Discourse Concerning the Holy Spirit* [1674], in *The Works of John Owen*, ed. William H. Goold [Edinburgh: Banner of Truth, 2004], 3:126). Why should *sanctifying grace* be common to both eras but not *communion-giving grace*?

Secondly, it is clear from a plain reading of the psalms that they *do* in fact express boldness and confidence in communion. Their authors 'feast on the abundance of [God's] house' (Ps. 36:8), find in him their 'exceeding joy' (Ps. 43:4) and 'take refuge under the shelter of [his] wings' (Ps. 61:4). In the many, many instances of the psalmists fervently enjoying the presence of God, *a priori* theological assumptions should not be employed to muzzle the text.

himself that eternal love or communion into which he would wish to introduce us too.'[11] Old covenant believers therefore lived with the awkwardness of singing without a Trinitarian consciousness acutely devotional songs which required a Trinitarian God. New covenant believers do not. Far from attempting to get back inside the heads of the original authors and be dictated by their theological outlook, new covenant believers celebrate possessing the key which at last makes the psalms explainable. We do not dispense with the Trinity when worshipping God through the psalms; it is the very truth which enables the psalms' relational vitality finally to make sense![12]

But it is one thing to establish in principle that the psalms — for the two reasons I have mentioned — should be used by Christians for Trinitarian devotion; it is another to know how that works in practice. As we have already observed, the psalms do not obviously divide into those

---

11. Dumitru Staniloae, *Orthodox Dogmatic Theology*, vol. 1, *The Experience of God* (Brookline, Massachusetts: Holy Cross Orthodox Press, 1994), 249.

12. The same point could be made concerning the Old Testament as a whole. The whole thing — with its highly covenantal structure — assumes a relational God; and the whole thing, therefore, is only really explainable with the Trinitarian consciousness of the new covenant believer. But it is in the Book of Psalms that the awkwardness of the old covenant situation is most acute.

It might well be asked, 'Why did God not relieve the awkwardness by revealing *sooner* his Trinitarian being?' The time-honoured answer to that question still has much to commend it: it was unsafe for God to do so given the pagan world his old covenant people inhabited and the proclivities they far too often demonstrated. In the words of Geerhardus Vos: 'Premature disclosure of the Trinity would in all probability have proved a temptation to polytheism' (Geerhardus Vos, *Biblical Theology: Old and New Testaments* [Edinburgh: Banner of Truth, 1975], 73).

which are peculiarly appropriate to communion with the Son, those which are peculiarly appropriate to communion with the Spirit, and those which are peculiarly appropriate to communion with the Father. One can only use the psalms for distinct communion by adopting a highly arbitrary approach — matching a particular psalm with a particular divine person according to whim rather than any intrinsic logic. Is that, then, the way we should proceed?

It is not. Rather, we apply to the psalms the form of Trinitarian devotion discussed earlier in this chapter. Through these inspired songs we glorify the one God, Father, Son and Holy Spirit — to use Torrance's formula once more. We address God neither conceiving of him as an impersonal essence, nor fastening onto a (randomly selected) single person of the Trinity. We address, instead, *the three together*. We do this knowing that in other contexts we might use the language of they-ness, but content in the psalms to adore the three using the language of he-ness.

Transitions

In part three of this book we shall consider the hypostatic transitions which, in my view, enrich Christian devotion — whereby one divine person is made, for a while, the focus of our communion, before a different divine person temporarily fills our vision, and so it goes on. Most of the material in parts one and two is paving the way, biblically and theologically, for the believer to engage with God in that hypostatically fluid manner.

This chapter has been different. Here, we have acknowledged that another, more basic transition is also appropriate to Christian devotion. Yes, the believer, engaging in distinct communion, oscillates between Father, Son and Spirit. But the believer also oscillates between distinct

communion itself and communion that is not distinct —
communion with the three together, the one tri-personal
God, addressed, perhaps, as 'God,' 'Yahweh' or 'Lord.'[13]

Or perhaps another singular form of address for the
three merits consideration, even if it can claim no biblical
precedent. I am struck by a phrase in Gregory Nazianzen's
famous speech as he relinquished the bishopric of
Constantinople. Having pleaded for Christian unity, and
that his ejection from the ecclesiastical ship might, Jonah-
like, still the storms of dispute, he then concludes:

> I reluctantly ascended the episcopal chair, and gladly I now
> come down. Even my weak body advises me this. One debt
> only have I to pay: death; this I owe to God. But, O my
> Trinity! for Thy sake only am I sad. Shalt Thou have an
> able man, bold and zealous to vindicate Thee? Farewell, and
> remember my labours and my pains.[14]

'O my Trinity!' Significantly, the phrase does not occur in a
context where the Cappadocian Father is discoursing on the
doctrine of God. It appears just to be a natural, intuitive way
for him to think and speak. And it is a lovely expression of
that indistinct communion, the validity of which has been
the burden of this chapter's slight detour. On the one hand,
Gregory's exclamation addresses the three persons *together*;
neither Father, Son, nor Spirit is made focal. On the other,
it does so with this term, 'Trinity,' which we invariably
associate with *persons*; its usage does not encourage a vague,
lazy, sub-personal conception of God.

---

13. Though the appellation, 'Lord,' used for the one tri-
personal God, is not without complication — since in the New
Testament it usually refers to Jesus specifically.

14. Philip Schaff, *History of the Christian Church: Nicene
and Post-Nicene Christianity*, vol. 3 (Edinburgh: T & T Clark,
1884), 919.

'Trinity' is an established term in our *theological* vocabulary. Perhaps, taking our cue from this fourth-century giant, we should preface the word with a first-person, possessive pronoun (singular in private contexts; plural in public settings) — and then make the resulting phrase a fixture in our *devotional* vocabulary. I think it would be a healthy, welcome development if the cry was heard more often in the contemporary evangelical church: 'O my/our Trinity!'

PART 2

THE THEOLOGICAL FRAMEWORK
OF DISTINCT COMMUNION

CHAPTER FOUR

The Search for Three Distinct Persons

In order to be tenable, the concept of distinct communion requires more than just a selection of sympathetic biblical texts. It requires a doctrine of the Trinity that is emphatic regarding the irreducible individuality of the Father and the Son and the Spirit. A theological framework is necessary in which the divine persons themselves are distinct enough to bear the weight of our distinct communion with them.

Two millennia of Trinitarian theology have bequeathed us a splendid array of principles and maxims. Many of these are strong assertions of the triune God's indivisibility. The dogma of *perichoresis* is in that category.[1] Its concern, prompted by Jesus' language in John's Gospel (10:38; 14:11; 17:21), is the complete unity of Father, Son and Spirit whereby each enfolds and accommodates the others within himself —

---

1. John of Damascus (*c.* 675–749) is widely credited with giving this term its Trinitarian meaning. According to Douglas Kelly, however, it was by St. Hilary, more than three centuries earlier, that the word 'was taken…to apply to the relationship in which the three divine persons mutually dwell in one another' (Douglas F. Kelly, *Systematic Theology*, vol. 1, *The God Who Is: The Holy Trinity* [Fearn, Ross-shire: Mentor, 2008], 489).

so that an encounter with any of the persons is, necessarily, an encounter with the three. *Perichoresis* is then built on by a further dogma, *opera trinitatis ad extra sunt indivisa* ('the external works of the Trinity are undivided'). Here, the persons' perichoretic inseparableness is extended to their *activities*. All that they do, they do *together*. They create and redeem as three perfectly intertwined agents — Father, Son and Spirit mutually involved in every divine operation.[2]

These assertions of indivisibility are glorious and indispensable. They ought to be defended tenaciously by every orthodox Trinitarian. But they do little to encourage distinct communion. Having confessed that Father, Son and Spirit wholly indwell one another (*perichoresis*), and that their actions are inseparable (the *opera ad extra*), it is hardly an obvious next step to conclude, 'And I relate to each of these persons in a way that is particular and distinguishable!'

Moreover, allied to this stress on indivisibility has been a further disincentive to distinct communion. When attention *has* been given to hypostatic distinctions in the being of God, those distinctions have often been depicted in a cold and uninviting way. The three persons, it seems, are distinguishable from each other by such features as unbegottenness, begottenness and procession. Terms like those might quicken the pulse of the theologian in his study, but they do little for the worshipper on his knees before the triune God. Donald Macleod aptly complains:

2. James Mackey finds an early expression of this idea in Gregory of Nyssa and his formula: 'The oneness of their nature must needs be inferred from *the identity of their operations*' (James P. Mackey, *The Christian Experience of God as Trinity* [London: SCM Press Ltd., 1983], 151 [italics mine]). The principle explains why the resurrection at the end of the age, for example, can be viewed in the New Testament either as the Father's work (1 Cor. 6:14) or as the Son's work (John 5:28-29) or as the Spirit's work (Rom. 8:11).

> The problem...is that although we know that the Son is distinguished by the fact that he is begotten, we know little or nothing of what divine begottenness is ... How does generation differ from procession? ... The truth is, we are lost.[3]

Why would a believer commune distinctly with persons whose distinctions are so abstract and lifeless?

How, then, has the concept of distinct communion managed to find any traction? Where have its exponents looked for their inspiration? If not to the great dogmas so concerned with indivisibility, and if not to the cumbersome 'distinguishing properties' classically attributed to the persons, then *where*?

Appropriations?

Perhaps the answer lies in the principle of *appropriations*.[4] This has been used to nuance the *opera ad extra*. It is the

---

3. Donald Macleod, *The Person of Christ* (Leicester: Inter-Varsity Press, 1998), 137-138. Gerald Bray is similarly frustrated with the unhelpfulness of these traditional distinctions. He sees it as a besetting flaw of fourth-century Cappadocian theology: 'The Cappadocians tended to make abstractions of words like "begotten" and "proceeding", thereby revealing a mental outlook basically foreign to that of Scripture. They turned relationships into attributes, and so invented qualities which do not exist. There is no such thing as "unbegottenness"; it is a category of thought which does not correspond to any observed reality distinct from the eternity which is shared by all three persons alike' (Gerald Bray, *The Doctrine of God* [Downers Grove, Illinois: Inter-Varsity Press, 1993], 163). And John Owen asks: 'Who can declare the generation of the Son, the procession of the Spirit, *or the difference of the one from the other?*' (John Owen, *Of the Mortification of Sin in Believers* [1658], in *The Works of John Owen*, ed. William H. Goold [Edinburgh: Banner of Truth, 2004], 6:67 [italics mine]).

4. It seems to have been in the thirteenth century that the language of *appropriations* started to become prominent. Mackey finds it in the writings of Thomas Aquinas (Mackey, op. cit., 182).

suggestion that while the persons are indeed inseparably involved in every divine work, they are not identically involved. Different aspects of the work are appropriated to each. It is not simply that Father, Son and Spirit together raise the dead on the Last Day (see fn. 2); rather, each person contributes to the resurrection event in his own way.

There is much merit in that approach. While it is difficult to delineate the distinct contributions of Father, Son and Spirit to the final resurrection, the principle of *appropriations* may successfully be applied to certain other works of God. The work of creation is an example. One of the most fascinating details of the Genesis 1 creation account is its fleeting, introductory reference to 'the Spirit of God' (Gen. 1:2).[5] We are surely to infer the Spirit's involvement in all that is subsequently narrated — otherwise the mention of him serves no purpose. And, given that he 'hover[s] over the face of the waters,' his involvement appears to be idiosyncratic. He is not the one issuing commands, forcing the heavens and earth into shape by his authoritative word. The Spirit's contribution, while perfectly in harmony with those resounding fiats, is distinct from them. B.B. Warfield captures the situation well:

> Over against the transcendent God, above creation, there seems to be postulated here God brooding upon creation, and the suggestion seems to be that it is only by virtue of God brooding upon creation that the created thing moves and acts and works out the will of God ... God's thought and

---

One sometimes encounters the same concept phrased instead in the language of *terminations*, the idea being that a divine operation, while involving all three, may *terminate* in one person.

5. I am assuming that *ruach elohim* in that text does mean 'the Spirit of God,' not, as has sometimes been suggested, 'a mighty wind'. Everywhere else in Genesis 1, *elohim* unambiguously refers to 'God'.

will and word take effect in the world, because God is not only over the world, thinking and willing and commanding, but also in the world … *executing.*[6]

In creation, then, God acts both transcendently (willing and commanding) and immanently (effecting and executing), and these different dimensions of the work are appropriated to different persons. The principle of *appropriations* thus seems pleasingly serviceable. Might this principle, concerned as it is with hypostatic distinctions, provide the theological launch pad for distinct communion? Might it illumine 'the splendour of the three' sufficiently to mould our devotional practice into a triadic shape? Might it drive the believer to seek a relationship with the Father *and* a relationship with the Son *and* a relationship with the Spirit?

Problems

Before embracing it too heartily, we need to appreciate the weaknesses in the principle of *appropriations.* Two problems in particular must be noted. First, there is a dizzying open-endedness about how the principle can be applied. Consider the following possibilities. We might select a narrowly focused work of God like the resurrection of the dead and try, hair-splittingly, to describe how one divine person's participation differs from another's. Then again, we might choose a more complex divine operation like the creation of the world and (with Warfield) appropriate clearly distinguishable strands of that activity to the different persons. Alternatively, however, we might step back and make creation itself the activity that is appropriated — it being one person's domain, while salvation is another's, and so on.

---

6. B.B. Warfield, 'The Spirit of God in the Old Testament,' in *Biblical and Theological Studies*, ed. Samuel G. Craig (Philadelphia, Pennsylvania: Presbyterian and Reformed, 1968), 134.

Thus, while the principle of *appropriations* is certainly interested in operational distinctness among the divine persons, the contours of that distinctness can look quite different in the hands of one theologian from how they look in the hands of another. This difficulty that one encounters in 'pinning down' the concept of *appropriations* limits its usefulness. Are we talking about a huge, discrete area of divine activity like *salvation* being assigned to a particular person? Or are we talking about the imperceptibly subtle distribution of roles that T.F. Torrance apparently has in mind:

> In every creative and redemptive act the Father, the Son and the Holy Spirit operate together in fellowship with one another but nevertheless in ways peculiar to each of them. *It is not possible for us to spell that out in terms of any demarcations between their distinctive operations.*[7]

A principle bathed in such ambiguity is hardly an ideal stimulus to distinct communion.

The second problem is that the *appropriations* principle simply lacks weight. It is not on an equal footing with the great expressions of indivisibility which dominate Trinitarian theology. One senses this in these words of Karl Barth:

> All God's work…is one act which occurs simultaneously and in concert in all His three modes of being. From creation… and reconciliation to the coming redemption it is always true that He who acts here is the Father and the Son and the Spirit. And it is true of all the perfections that are to be declared in relation to this work of God that they are as much the perfections of the Father as of the Son and the

---

7. Thomas F. Torrance, *The Christian Doctrine of God, One Being Three Persons* (Edinburgh: T & T Clark, 2006), 198 (italics mine).

Spirit. *Per appropriationem* this act or this attribute must now be given prominence in relation to this or that mode of being in order that this can be described as such. But only *per appropriationem* may this happen.[8]

There is a reluctant tone to those last two sentences. They leave questions in the reader's mind. When Scripture appropriates an act or attribute to a 'mode of being' (a divine person), does that correspond to anything in the realm of objective reality? Can the appropriation be taken at face value? It is not clear from Barth's comments that it can. The association of certain acts with certain persons appears somehow to be necessary for the purposes of revelation, but the truer fact lying behind the appropriation to the one is the concerted action of the three. The primary truth, it seems, is that every work of God involves all the persons; the foregrounding of a particular person with reference to a particular work occurs only at a secondary level.

There is nothing to suggest that Barth's understanding of appropriations is atypical. Certainly, he does not think it so. He briefly surveys how Aquinas, Bonaventura, Luther and Calvin appropriate aspects of divine activity to the persons,[9] and he considers himself to be expounding the same doctrine as they. It appears, then, that in most of its varied expressions from the thirteenth to the twentieth centuries, the principle of appropriations does not function as a bold assertion of the persons' distinguishable operations. Its status is not that of a non-negotiable dogma, fundamental to our doctrine of the Trinity. It is a concession. It merely qualifies statements of divine unity and indivisibility which are more substantial

---

8. Karl Barth, *Church Dogmatics*, ed. Thomas F. Torrance and Geoffrey W. Bromiley, trans. Geoffrey W. Bromiley (Edinburgh: T & T Clark, 1956), I/1: 374-375.

9. Ibid., 373.

than it. Robert Jenson concludes that 'The doctrine [of appropriations] is either empty or modalistic.'[10] One may balk at the directness of Jenson's charge, but it is difficult to deny that it contains some truth.

Agents of Salvation

We may grant that the principle of appropriations moves in the right direction. To the perceptive believer it might just suggest a radical idea: that divine persons who act distinguishably ought to be known and loved distinctly. But the suggestion is faint and inchoate. Our doctrine of the Trinity needs to offer a more substantial foundation on which the edifice of distinct communion may rest. Something concrete is required. Appropriations, as they have been treated in Trinitarian theology, are not enough.

The predominant theme of the entire Bible is God's accomplishing of salvation. One of the most remarkable summaries of that salvation is Paul's in Galatians 4:4-6:

> But when the fullness of time had come, God sent forth his Son, born of woman, born under the law, to redeem those who were under the law, so that we might receive adoption as sons. And because you are sons, God has sent the Spirit of his Son into our hearts, crying, 'Abba! Father!'

Paul writes there of two 'sendings,' two saving missions. The Son is sent, and the Spirit is sent; and the unsent sender is in both cases God (the Father). In a stroke this text takes us beyond the constricted parameters of appropriations. Here we are confronted with a variation of activity among the persons far more pronounced than anything which that principle envisages. An appropriation, Barth insists,

---

10. Robert W. Jenson, *Systematic Theology*, vol. 1, *The Triune God* (New York: Oxford University Press, 1997), 113.

'must not be exclusive.... What is appropriated belongs in fact to all the modes of being'.[11] But these saving operations of Father, Son and Spirit in Galatians 4:4-6 are exclusive! The exclusiveness is not, of course, total: other Scriptures reveal that in each person's saving activity there is certainly participation by the others. But the exclusiveness is profound. The Father and Spirit are not sent to be born of woman under the law; it is the preserve of the Son. The Father and Son are not sent into our hearts crying, 'Abba! Father!'; the Spirit alone plays that part. Neither the Son nor the Spirit is an unsent sender; only the Father fits that description. There are unshared roles here, differences of redemptive action which quite simply are irreducible.

At last, then, we have an answer to our question. Where, we asked, do we find a doctrine of the Trinity that upholds the persons' distinctness so robustly as to invite distinct communion? We find it in God's work of saving sinners! We view the Trinity there; and the spectacle of these three agents of salvation, each involved in such a radically particular manner, animates the desire to relate in different ways to them all.

Robert Letham writes boldly: 'It is often said that the only distinction of the persons is the ineffable eternal generation and procession. This is not so.' Letham goes on to describe how the Father, the Son and the Spirit each assume a saving role which the other two do not. He considers these differences of redemptive action to be as determinative as anything else for our conception of the triune God. And he thus has no qualms about making them the basis of our relationship to God: 'We might ask whether this irreducible distinctiveness lends sharpness to our worship.'[12]

---

11. Barth, *Church Dogmatics*, I/1: 374.
12. Robert Letham, *The Holy Trinity: In Scripture, History,*

But is it proper to derive our understanding of the triune God from how we see him saving sinners? It might be the case that he redeems his people in a highly person-specific way, but is it right to extrapolate from that? Is it legitimate to embed salvation's demarcations within our doctrine of the Trinity? There are two possible objections.

The Economic Trinity

First, it might be objected that this leans too heavily on the so-called *economic Trinity*. While the *immanent Trinity* is the divine persons in their eternal engagement solely with each other, the economic Trinity is the divine persons in their engagement with the created order. It is God acting outside of himself.

It is a fundamental tenet of orthodox theology that all God's activities outside of himself are discretionary. His being is in no way dependent upon his creative and redemptive projects. Those external works may be removed from the picture, yet God is not less. His existence quite apart from them, and irrespective of them, is complete, optimal and unimpaired. And that being so, the argument goes, God's works ought not to be the basis of our Trinitarian conclusions. The Trinity as it is in the economy ought not to be our concern, but rather the Trinity as it is eternally and essentially. Only those distinctions between the persons which transcend God's engagement with the created order are relevant to our doctrine of God — hence the preoccupation, mentioned earlier, with *begottenness*, *unbegottenness* and *procession*. Distinguishing the persons according to those 'properties' is valid; distinctions relating to their saving roles, on the other hand, do not count.

Theology, and Worship (Phillipsburg, N.J.: P&R Publishing, 2004), 418 (italics mine).

This objection, however, is far from unanswerable. A willingness to lean heavily on the economic Trinity is in fact eminently defensible. It is not (or at least need not be) a denial of God's aseity and separateness from the creation. It is rather an affirmation of his faithfulness and consistency. It assumes that in his external works the triune God is true to himself. Hypostatic distinctions are neither deepened nor diminished as the Trinity embarks upon salvation; they remain what they are. The God of the incarnation and the cross is an authentic version of his eternal self. Between the Trinity as it simply is and the Trinity in action, there is complete continuity.

Indeed, if the revelatory value of the economy is discounted, belief in the Trinity itself may well be imperilled. Peter Robinson makes some important points about Karl Rahner's famous aphorism that the economic Trinity is the immanent Trinity and the immanent Trinity is the economic Trinity. Robinson helpfully remarks:

> 'Rahner's Rule' overturns the assumption that, while the three hypostases are true to God *ad extra*, God *ad intra* is a simple undifferentiated essence or *ousia* … [It] forced us to recognise the way in which the Trinitarian affirmation of the One and the Three became confused with the distinction between *theologia* and *economia*.[13]

This 'assumption' to which he refers — and which, he implies, was in Rahner's crosshairs — is a deeply disturbing one. It demonstrates that the gulf in our theology between the immanent God and the economic God, if the revelatory

---

13. Peter M.B. Robinson, 'The Trinity: The Significance of Appropriate Distinctions for Dynamic Relationality,' in *Trinitarian Soundings in Systematic Theology*, ed. Paul Louis Metzger (London: T & T Clark, 2006), 53-54.

significance of the latter is not appreciated, can become very wide indeed. If salvation is designated an unreliable window into the being of God, then why should not the distinctions of Father, Son and Spirit themselves be unreal? Why not conclude that in a mere temporary deviation from his ontological state, God undertakes redemption as three persons? Why not dismiss the divine tripersonality as an inessential arrangement adopted for reasons of expedience? After all, our other windows on God are exceedingly small. The attempt to view him without reference to the economy, making use only of Scripture's direct, non-soteriological disclosures, does not yield much. Such an exiguous 'revelation' of God is hardly calculated to dazzle us with 'the splendour of the three'; and it may just be amenable to the suggestion that, actually, in his truest and most essential form God is monadic. If we close salvation's revelatory window, we may lose Father, Son and Spirit altogether. If, on the other hand, the window is left open, we not only *have* these three persons but must reckon with their striking distinctness.

Propositional Revelation

The second objection to viewing the Trinity through salvation's window levels this charge: it involves an undermining of propositional revelation. God is a precise communicator. Precise communication necessitates tight, verbal propositions in which the scope for misunderstanding is minimal. Thus, God reveals the most important truths about himself in that form. He uses what Paul Helm calls 'one-liners,' crisp assertions like these: 'God is spirit' (John 4:24); 'God is one' (Rom. 3:30); 'The Lord looks on the heart' (1 Sam. 16:7); 'The Father has life in himself' (John 5:26); 'Jesus Christ is the same yesterday and today and

THE SEARCH FOR THREE DISTINCT PERSONS

for ever' (Heb. 13:8).[14] It is primarily from this sort of biblical material, then, that we are to derive our doctrine of God. Doing so, moreover, lies at the heart of systematic theology: its business is the organising of these great propositions into coherent doctrines — whether of creation, of man, of sin, of Christ, of the church, of the eschaton, or, indeed, of God.

By contrast salvation, the argument proceeds, is unsuited to giving us doctrine. Salvation is a series of events, the unfolding of a narrative. Events and narrative involve ambiguities. They lack dogmatism. Timeless statements must take precedence. To make salvation's storyline determinative for our doctrine of the Trinity is to slight propositional revelation and the discipline of systematic theology which specialises in it.

But this objection, too, fails to overturn the case we are making. In actual fact, to go to salvation for our Trinitarian theology is not to renounce dependence upon propositional revelation. It is true that salvation is events, but the biblical narration of those events itself involves unambiguous, verbal statements. Insofar as we conclude from the Son's incarnation and the Spirit's outpouring that the divine persons are profoundly distinct, we are deriving our doctrine of God from events. But how do we know that the conception of that embryo in Mary's womb is the incarnation of the Son? We know it because of the angel Gabriel's declaration to that effect. And how do we know that the series of phenomena on the day of Pentecost is the outpouring of the Spirit? We know it because of Jesus' declarations in advance, not to mention Peter's declarations on the day itself. Apart from these precise, verbal articulations, the pregnancy in Nazareth and the

---

14. Paul Helm, *Faith, Form, and Fashion: Classical Reformed Theology and Its Postmodern Critics* (Cambridge: James Clarke & Co, 2014), 93.

eruption of glossolalia in Jerusalem are unintelligible. They reveal nothing of the triune God. Thus, the suggestion is not that narrative material should replace declarative material as an alternative source of revelation. The two are friends, not enemies. To submit to salvation's disclosure of the Trinity is, necessarily, to submit to the numerous propositions woven into the fabric of that disclosure.

More importantly, however, it is simply a matter of observation that the Bible's abstract statements are not its main channel of Trinitarian revelation. Such statements may serve the theologian well when an inventory of God's moral characteristics is being compiled: the divine love, faithfulness, justice, wisdom, holiness and power all receive abundant support from them. But they prove considerably less serviceable when the divine triune nature is being probed. Helm's long list of 'one-liners' — far more extensive than the small sample I cited above — appears to confirm this. Reference to God's triune nature is reserved by Helm for an unsatisfactory footnote appended to the list: 'Other statements could be added, having to do with his Trinitarian nature'.[15] Even if one assumes, charitably, that these 'other statements' are indeed waiting in the wings, omitted by Helm in the interests of brevity, the omission is suggestive: God's

---

15. Ibid., 93. It is only fair that Helm's motives for writing on the theme of propositional revelation should be noted. He does not engage in the book with those like Warfield and Owen (both of whom are quoted below) who see the Trinity revealed narratively in Scripture; quite possibly, he would have no problem with their approach. Rather, it is with those contemporary evangelicals who have little or no interest in systematic theology that Helm takes issue. That is an understandable concern, and against such a backdrop, one sympathises with his zeal for 'classical reformed theology.' But in my view his championing of biblical 'one-liners' is too absolute and, perhaps inadvertently, conflicts with the methodology of historic orthodoxy's greatest Trinitarians.

'Trinitarian nature,' it would seem, is absent from the Bible's leading, first on the list, most readily quotable one-liners. The natural conclusion to be drawn is that the Trinity is a minor doctrine! If, however, that conclusion is unthinkable, then the whole method of viewing God primarily through abstract propositions is flawed. Perhaps God has in fact revealed the most important truth about himself through the storyline of salvation.

B.B. Warfield is convinced that he has. According to Warfield:

> We cannot speak of the doctrine of the Trinity, therefore, if we study exactness of speech, as revealed in the New Testament, any more than we can speak of it as revealed in the Old Testament…. The revelation…was made not in word but in deed … This is as much as to say that the revelation of the Trinity was incidental to, and the inevitable effect of, the accomplishment of redemption.[16]

Gazing through salvation's window is not a crime against propositional revelation. It is simply the recognition that, when it comes to his tripersonality, God has unveiled himself 'not in word but in deed.'

The Convergence in Owen

Warfield is not being novel. Others before him had stressed 'deed' as the primary arena in which the tri-personal God reveals himself. In fact, John Owen insists upon it in such similar terms to those of Warfield that it could appear redundant for me to quote the Puritan. Is there anything to be gained by highlighting another affirmation of event-

---

16. B.B. Warfield, 'The Biblical Doctrine of the Trinity,' in *Biblical and Theological Studies*, ed. Samuel G. Craig (Philadelphia, Pennsylvania: Presbyterian and Reformed, 1968), 32-33.

focused Trinitarian revelation which differs so little from the one offered by Warfield more than two centuries later? There is. The justification for hearing Owen's voice, too, in this connection will follow the quote itself:

> The great work whereby God designed to glorify himself ultimately in this world was that of the *new creation*, or of the recovery and restoration of all things by Jesus Christ…. That which God ordereth and designeth as the principal means for the manifestation of his glory must contain the most perfect and absolute *revelation* and declaration of himself…. In particular, in this new creation he hath revealed himself in an especial manner as *three in one*…. And this was done not so much in express propositions or verbal testimonies unto that purpose…as by the declaration of the mutual, divine, internal acts of the persons towards one another, and the distinct, immediate, divine, external actings of each person in the work which they did and do perform, — for God revealeth not himself unto us merely doctrinally and dogmatically, but by the declaration of what he doth for us, in us, and towards us…[17]

Owen, like Warfield after him, unashamedly constructs his doctrine of the Trinity from an examination of what God 'doth for us'; he privileges redemption above 'propositions or verbal testimonies' as our window on the triune God. But Owen's doing so is of particular importance because, as we have seen previously, this same theologian also urges the vigorous pursuit of tri-personal devotion. In Owen, then, a soteriologically-shaped understanding of the Trinity and a commitment to distinct communion converge. And that convergence is not an unexplainable coincidence. The divine

---

17. John Owen, *A Discourse Concerning the Holy Spirit* (1674), in *The Works of John Owen*, ed. William H. Goold (Edinburgh: Banner of Truth, 2004), 3:157-58.

persons in Owen's Trinitarian theology are the Father, Son, and Spirit of the gospel, collaborators in a complex saving project which requires the unique, non-interchangeable contribution of each; it is therefore entirely natural for Owen to relate to the different persons in commensurately unique and non-interchangeable ways. In his doctrine of the Trinity, derived from redemption's epic saga, Father, Son and Spirit are conspicuously distinct; consistency demands that the same degree of distinctness should apply in the realm of devotion.

We have found, then, our theological launch pad for distinct communion: a doctrine of the Trinity in which the persons' distinctions are substantial enough to bear the weight of this devotional practice. It is the doctrine of the Trinity revealed in salvation. But just how substantial *are* the distinctions on display as God acts to save his people? We have already noted that in Galatians 4:4-6 each person appears to perform in turn a role that is peculiarly his. Barth, however, is keen to restrain the conclusions we make from the storyline of redemption. He cautions that 'It would be pagan mythology to present the work of God in the form of a dramatic entry and exit of now one and now another of the divine persons'.[18] Are we, then, being too cavalier when we speak of salvation's three agents performing distinguishable roles? Are we no longer operating within the boundaries of biblical monotheism? And, consequently, are we basing the concept of distinct communion on an understanding of the saving God that is in fact faulty and paganised?

In my view the more relevant question is this: what redemption is Barth looking at, that he is able to pour cold water on the idea of distinct hypostatic agents performing distinct roles? Is it really the redemption narrated in the

---

18. Barth, *Church Dogmatics*, I/1: 374.

New Testament? Donald Macleod comments judiciously that 'We must not let an *a priori* fear of tritheism come between us and the biblical data.'[19] In the story of the incarnation and ascension of the Son and Pentecostal descent of the Spirit, the biblical data depict something much closer to 'a dramatic entry and exit of now one and now another' than Barth's fear of tritheism will allow him to concede. It is he who misrepresents the gospel as a rather faceless programme executed by three 'modes of being'; it is not Owen (and others of his persuasion) who misrepresent it as an overly hypostasised, mythological drama. The latter are right to see displayed in salvation personal distinctions that are truly profound — profound enough, indeed, to shape our entire communion with God.

We shall begin the next chapter by focusing on one of the person's saving roles, one of the 'sendings' of Galatians 4 — namely, the mission of the Son. There we shall encounter evidence of remarkable personal individuality, confirmation that the practice of distinct communion does indeed rest on a firm foundation.

---

19. Macleod, *Person of Christ*, 126.

CHAPTER FIVE

Gazing Through Salvation's Window

The Incarnation of the Son

The great story of history is the story of God saving a people for himself. And as he engages in that project, the deliverance of innumerable human beings from sin and hell is not the only outcome. It also entails a revelation. It affords unparalleled views of God. And the God we see in this salvation drama is three persons; and the three persons we see are arrestingly distinct. It is that sight which, more than anything else, conduces to the differentiated pursuit of Father, Son and Spirit which is the theme of this book.

We shall now allow ourselves to take in that sight. Or at least, we shall focus on one of the divine persons in his saving activities: we shall consider the Son. Of course, it is as the Son performs his saving role that he bequeaths us our greatest statements of the persons' unity: 'I and the Father are one' (John 10:30); 'The Father is in me and I am in the Father' (John 10:38); 'Whoever has seen me has seen the Father' (John 14:9). But to concentrate exclusively on those — as though the Son's mission contributes little more to our Trinitarian theology than a few verbal reinforcements of divine indivisibility — would be an indefensibly blinkered approach. For one of the most striking features of those statements is the fact they emanate from a pair of lips and a set of vocal cords! The one claiming this indivisible unity with the Father is a Galilean man, standing on an ordinary piece of Middle Eastern soil as he does so. Elsewhere, he insists that the Father is 'in heaven' (Matt. 6:9), is 'spirit' (John 4:24), and is beyond the reach of human sight (John 1:18). None of that is true of himself. He is patently on earth, composed of flesh and blood, and exposed to the eyes of all! He inhabits a set of conditions quite different from the conditions the Father inhabits. Thus, while the stunning claims which bedeck his mission do indeed point to an inseparable, perichoretic oneness with the Father, the truth more conspicuously on display every single moment of this very human, very this-worldly mission is his distinctness from the Father. To accept the most obvious thing about the saving Son — that he is incarnate — is to accept something that has never been (and never will be) true of the other divine persons.

This reality draws from John Owen one of the boldest remarks he ever pens. He contends that 'the susception of the human nature by the Son, and all that he did therein' represents 'a peculiar condescension of [a divine] person unto a work, wherein the other [divine persons] have no concurrence but by approbation and consent.'[1] Of course, that sentence must not be abused. Owen is not suggesting that any of the persons were uninvolved in the Son's

---

1. John Owen, *A Discourse Concerning the Holy Spirit* (1674), in *The Works of John Owen*, ed. William H. Goold (Edinburgh: Banner of Truth, 2004), 3:94. He later remarks: 'There is such a distinction in their operations, that one divine act may produce a peculiar respect and relation unto one person, *and not unto another*' (ibid., 162; italics mine).

incarnation. Few theologians in the history of the church have stressed more than he the role of the Spirit, for instance, in relation to it — a point to which we shall return in chapter seven. When writing these words, however, Owen does not have in mind the facilitating or enabling or maintaining of the incarnation — all of which, it can be argued, depend upon the participation of the other persons. Here, it is the experience itself of being incarnate that fills his purview. And for him the closest the Father and the Spirit come to that is offering their 'approbation and consent' — which is not very close at all! Undergoing incarnation is as foreign to the Father and Spirit as the experiences of committing a sin or having a memory lapse are! Neither of those persons knows from the inside what it is to exist humanly. We are dealing here with a stark, intra-Trinitarian asymmetry, an irreducible divergence within the Godhead, a point of 'no concurrence' (to repeat Owen's phrase) at the heart of the triune God: a non-incarnate Father, a non-incarnate Spirit, and an incarnate Son.

Some of the theological implications of this asymmetry are open to debate. Does it render the *opera ad extra* dogma unfit for purpose? That depends upon how tightly one defines 'undivided works.' Perhaps it is legitimate to define them loosely enough that a Son who becomes incarnate and a Father who does not are still working undividedly. Owen appears content to do so. Despite his bold words on the incarnation cited above, he always writes approvingly of the *opera ad extra* — though some suspect the Puritan here of both having his cake and eating it![2]

2. Alan Spence is one theologian unconvinced by Owen's both/and approach. He contends that '[Owen's] theology... requires a modification of the *opera Trinitatis ad extra sunt indivisa*' (Alan Spence, *Incarnation and Inspiration: John Owen*

But whether or not it can be said that an incarnate Son and a non-incarnate Father are 'working undividedly' in the way the ancient dogma meant it, what cannot be said is a remark like this: 'When I deal with Christ, and think of Christ, I must think I have to deal with the Father. Christ was incarnate; it was as much as if the Father had been incarnate.'[3] That is a refusal to face up to the basic facts of

and the Coherence of Christology [London: T & T Clark, 2007], 144). But cf. Tyler R. Wittman, 'The End of the Incarnation: John Owen, Trinitarian Agency and Christology,' International Journal of Systematic Theology 15 (2013), for a spirited defence of Owen's fidelity to the dogma.

Perhaps Owen felt no need to reconcile in a comprehensively logical manner the opera ad extra with the Father and Spirit's 'no concurrence' in the incarnation. He does, after all, comment in one place that 'Many things are above reason ... which are not at all against it ... There is no concernment of the being of God, or his properties, but is absolutely above the comprehension of our reason ... It is the highest reason in things of pure revelation to captivate our understandings to the authority of the Revealer' (John Owen, A Brief Declaration and Vindication of the Doctrine of the Holy Trinity [1668-1669], in The Works of John Owen, ed. William H. Goold [Edinburgh: Banner of Truth, 2004], 2:412).

Although it cannot be explored here, it is fascinating to observe that this Owenian tension in the realm of God's works resurfaces in the realm of God's will. There, too, the Puritan juxtaposes statements of unity and statements of distinctness. He makes this extraordinary statement: 'This will is appropriated to them respectively, so that the will of the Father and the will of the Son may be considered distinctly' (John Owen, The Mystery of the Gospel Vindicated and Socinianism Examined [1655], in The Works of John Owen, ed. William H. Goold [Edinburgh: Banner of Truth, 2004], 12:497). It is important to be clear he is not here alluding to the human will of the incarnate Son. He is in fact discussing a pre-temporal covenant between Father and Son: the eternal Son willed a set of covenantal undertakings that were not the same as those willed by the eternal Father.

3. Richard Sibbes, A Christian's Portion; or, The Christian's Charter, in The Works of Richard Sibbes, ed. Alexander B. Grosart

the salvation drama. The Father did not become incarnate. On that point there can be no debate. To suggest, however well-meaningly, that the Father did in some sense become incarnate is to play fast and loose with the biblical gospel. The hypostatic individuality involved in the incarnation must simply be accepted. And it must then compel the acknowledgement: if the divine persons can diverge on such a consequential point as the possession of human nature, then those persons are profoundly distinct.

His Prayers

When viewing the Son at work in salvation, we soon encounter further indications of personal distinctness. The bare fact of his incarnate state is not the only point of interest.

It is clear from the gospel narratives that the incarnate Son prayed. Prayer, indeed, appears to have featured prominently as he undertook his mission. But to whom did he pray? Though ostensibly a bland question, its significance is thrown into relief by a remark that Karl Rahner makes. He states that, 'Kerygmatically it would be incorrect to dwell on the fact that Jesus worshipped the Son of God.'[4] Rahner is making a point about preaching: the notion of Jesus directing his prayers to God the Son does not reflect

---

(Edinburgh: Banner of Truth, 1983), 4:36. Interestingly, in the very same breath Sibbes also says that the incarnation 'was by [the Father's] authority' (ibid., 4:36). At that point he is basically in agreement with Owen, merely substituting 'authority' for Owen's comparable term, 'consent.' For both these Puritans, then, the Father's role in the incarnation consists in giving his imprimatur. But whereas for Owen that imprimatur merely qualifies slightly the Father's *non-concurrence* in the incarnation, for Sibbes it signifies such a *concurrence* that, effectively, the Father becomes incarnate, too!

4. K. Rahner, *Theological Investigations*, vol. 1 (London: Darton, Longman & Todd Ltd., 1961), 129.

the 'modes of expression current in the New Testament'[5] and ought not to be verbalised in Christian proclamation. The assumption behind his point, however, is that Jesus did indeed direct his prayers to God the Son. For Rahner that is a 'fact'; the only issue is whether or not the preacher should 'dwell on' it.

But his assumption must surely be rejected. Jesus cannot have prayed to the Son. That would leave us with a divided, Nestorian Christ. If his human nature could interact with his divine nature in an I-thou kind of relationship, then the incarnation is not the union of two natures in one person. Rather, the natures themselves possess personal properties, and Christ becomes a deeply unstable dual personality. The saving accomplishments which Christian piety has attributed to a single, unified agent, the God-man Christ Jesus, must instead be attributed to a pair of natures, each with its own individual agency. Rahner himself does not venture along that logical trajectory; he always writes as though Christ's existential unity were a given. Nonetheless, it *is* the logical trajectory of his assumption that Jesus directed his prayers to God the Son.

The necessary alternative, then, is that the objects of Jesus' prayers were the Father and the Spirit. If we are to maintain the integrity of the incarnate Christ, the Son must be excluded as an object. Admittedly, we are venturing into that theological hinterland where revelation gives way to impenetrable mystery. We must respect that there are limits to what is humanly analysable. But the observation that Jesus prayed only to the Father and Spirit permits this conclusion at least: for such discriminating prayers to be possible, the divine persons must be notably distinct.

---

5. Ibid., 129.

Again, then, by viewing the Son in his saving work —
in this case the often-overlooked area of his prayer life
therein — we are forced to recognise the depth of personal
distinctness inherent in the triune God.

The Cross

We cannot view the Son in his saving work without
considering its climax. It was ultimately at the cross that he
accomplished his people's redemption. This was the goal of
his incarnation: he assumed flesh and blood precisely so that
on Good Friday he could suffer and die (Heb. 2:14).

And if the cross was the climactic point of his saving work,
the climactic point of the cross was the ninth hour cry, 'My
God, my God, why have you forsaken me?' (Matt. 27:46; Mark
15:34). That anguished utterance is perhaps the greatest clue
within the event itself as to the meaning of Christ's ordeal.
Isaiah had foretold the event in terms of Yahweh crushing
the victim (Isa. 53:10), and Paul would later reflect on the
propitiatory nature of Christ's suffering (Rom. 3:25). But the
cry of dereliction is the sufferer's own testimony to the pre-
eminent truth about Golgotha: God the Father was acting in
vengeance, punishing his Son for the sins of others.

And that punishment was in the form of abandonment:
the Son was 'forsaken'. Once again, the sense of mystery
here is acute, and we must beware prying irreverently
into that which is inscrutable. But the Son's experience of
abandonment, though veiled to a significant degree, is not
altogether beyond the reach of theological analysis. It is
legitimate to relate the cross to a persistent theme running
through the Bible. Repeatedly in the Scriptures, the inflicting
of divine wrath involves the concept of removal.

This motif may be traced all the way from the eviction of
our disgraced first parents, through Cain's banishment and

Israel's Babylonian exile, to 'the great divorce' (to use C.S. Lewis' phrase) of the *eschaton*. Regarding the latter, the New Testament could scarcely be more emphatic. It insists that the damned will finally be 'outside' (Rev. 22:15), 'cast out' (Luke 13:28); they will 'go away' (Matt. 25:46), consigned to a remote and distant 'outer darkness' (Matt. 25:30). That final removal from the presence of God is not, of course, absolute: the damned do not cease to exist; and if existent, they cannot be entirely independent of God.[6] But the removal is real. The biblical references are too abundant and too unqualified for the concept to be dismissed as poetic hyperbole.

And such removal, then, must have been the experience of the Son at Golgotha. The iniquities of myriad human beings had been laid on him (Isa. 53:6). He had been made sin (2 Cor. 5:21). Consequently, there never was a more eligible candidate than he to be expelled from God's presence. Though in a sense treasuring his Son as never before (for Christ had voluntarily contracted his people's guilt in an act of filial obedience), the Father could not righteously tolerate this sin-bearer. Like the goat in the Day of Atonement ritual, he must be driven out to far-flung regions where he could offend no more the One 'of purer eyes than to see evil' (Hab. 1:13). In the language of the Creed, he must descend into hell.

---

6. Thomas Goodwin points out that if the inhabitants of hell remain in a biological sense alive, they must be sustained by God. He speaks of 'a double expense of power'. 'At the same instant (and that lengthened out for ever) God sets himself by his power to destroy the creature utterly, in respect of its wellbeing; whilst yet again, on the other hand, as great a power is requisite to uphold it in being and sense, and to prevent its sinking into its first nothing, or from failing before him, in respect of being [able] to bear it' (Thomas Goodwin, *An Unregenerate Man's Guiltiness before God, in Respect of Sin and Punishment*, in *The Works of Thomas Goodwin* [Edinburgh: James Nichol, 1865], 10:499).

Truly, therefore, he was forsaken. The ninth hour cry reveals more than just Christ's psychological state. This is no mere subjective loss of assurance, a wretched set of circumstances conspiring to overwhelm his consciousness and exclude all happier considerations. His words express, rather, an objective reality: he has been subjected to penal removal. For a brief but terrible period of time, 'Adam's sins have swept between the righteous Son and Father'[7] — and with those sins, all the wrath due to them. Christ utters a cry of dereliction because in that moment he is derelict.

And the possibility of a derelict, abandoned Son has momentous Trinitarian implications. It indicates a distinctness among the divine persons that is weighty and unmistakable; a distinctness that is brilliantly illuminated that Friday afternoon at Golgotha but that cannot have originated there. It is true, of course, that the interposition of sin and wrath within the Father and Son's relationship is an extraordinary, unprecedented twist in the story of reality. Donald Macleod, reflecting on sin as ἀνομία (*anomia*) (1 John 3:4), captures well the sheer inconceivableness of Calvary: 'Here is the final anomalousness of sin. Impossible in itself, its existence immediately creates the possibility of further impossibilities, climaxing in the accursedness of the Son and the pain of the Father.'[8] Sin can create terrible new possibilities; it can create the unthinkable situation in which one divine person becomes the object of another's curse and wrath. But even sin cannot tamper with the deepest structures of the Trinity, making the persons more distinct than they otherwise were. Certainly, without sin's

---

7. From the poem 'Cowper's Grave' by Elizabeth Barrett Browning (1806-1861).

8. Donald Macleod, *The Person of Christ* (Leicester: Inter-Varsity Press, 1998), 177.

emergence, the notion of the Son being penally removed from the Father would have remained the out of the question absurdity it ought ever to have been. But the degree of personal distinctness necessary for that penal removal would have existed, nonetheless. Sin cannot claim the credit for that! It must rather be intrinsic, built into the very fabric of the triune God.

It is interesting in this connection to consult some of those writers most zealously committed to the persons' 'inseparable operations.' Golgotha's drama does appear awkwardly resistant to that rubric. These authors have to represent the central event of our faith in a form which at times feels unrecognisable. For Adonis Vidu, the persons' sharing of every external work is so total that the atonement cannot possibly involve one acting in wrath against another: 'The Father does not…punish the incarnate Word, since this involves an action of God terminating in a created effect (the human nature of Jesus). But any such action of God…must be actions common to the three.'[9] Bruce McCormack moves in the same direction but is keen to preserve the notion of an outpouring of wrath. This leads him to the following conclusion:

> The subject who delivers Jesus Christ up to death is not the Father alone. For the trinitarian axiom *opera trinitatis ad extra sunt indivisa* means that if one does it, they all do it … And that also means, then, that the Father is not doing something to someone other than himself. The triune God pours his wrath out upon himself.[10]

9. Adonis Vidu, 'The Place of the Cross Among the Inseparable Operations of the Trinity,' in *Locating Atonement: Explorations in Constructive Dogmatics*, ed. Oliver D. Crisp and Fred Sanders (Grand Rapids, Michigan: Zondervan, 2015), 40.

10. Bruce L. McCormack, 'The Ontological Presuppositions of

That is an extraordinary construal of the cross. According to Paul, God 'did not spare his own Son' (Rom. 8:32). In McCormack's treatment, however, that moving story is rewritten. We no longer have a tender Father reluctantly yet resolutely afflicting his beloved Son. We are left, instead, with this cumbersome scenario of the Trinity pouring its wrath on the Trinity![11] Surely it is preferable to retain the New Testament's plain account of God the Father in wrath abandoning God the Son; and to acknowledge, consequently, that these persons must be sufficiently distinct for such penal removal to invade their relationship. And if that necessitates the addition of more nuance to our doctrine of 'inseparable operations,' then so be it.

Barth's Doctrine of the Atonement,' in *The Glory of the Atonement: Biblical, Historical and Practical Perspectives*, ed. Charles E. Hill and Frank A. James III (Downers Grove, Illinois: Inter-Varsity Press, 2004), 364.

11. It is a prime example of a phenomenon described by Brian Kay: 'An over-emphasis on divine unity, among other things, is a drama killer, for three actors are reduced to one, and the moving interplay between them in their enacted conspiracy to redeem their people is lost' (Brian Kay, *Trinitarian Spirituality: John Owen and the Doctrine of God in Western Devotion* [Milton Keynes: Paternoster, 2007], 41).

Interestingly, McCormack sees his approach as necessary for defending the *morality* of penal substitution: 'A well-ordered penal substitution theory (one that gets its ontological presuppositions right) does not portray this event in terms of a violent action of God (conceived of as one individual) upon his Son (conceived of as a second distinct individual). ...and the moral charge against penal substitution cannot finally be sustained' (McCormack, op. cit., 365). But if the Son had become the willing bearer of his people's sins, that alone is sufficient to counter the moral charge. The vindication of penal substitution resides in the very fact that it is *penal substitution* (not the arbitrary infliction of suffering). De-emphasising the participants' individualities is not required.

We have touched, then, on several areas: the basic fact that the Son, uniquely, became incarnate; the way in which his prayers, necessarily, were directed to some and not all of the persons of the Godhead; and the experience of dereliction he suffered at the cross. These are a few of the vistas that emerge as the Son undertakes his redemptive activity, and they bear common testimony to a Trinity of profound hypostatic distinctions. Having taken in these vistas, it is difficult to disagree with Macleod's assessment:

> There can be little doubt, if we take Scripture as our guide, that the distinctions within the Godhead are analogous to those which obtain between individual human beings. The Father, the Son and the Spirit act not only *with* each other but *on* each other. Each is both conscious and self-conscious, and each plays a distinctive and unique role in redemption. That at least is the impression we gain from the New Testament …[12]

The conclusions of the previous chapter are thus reinforced. The stark tripersonality of the saving God warrants the practice of distinct communion. The three agents of our salvation are markedly differentiated. They are persons of sufficient individuality as to invite an individual relationship with each. It is entirely reasonable that our communion with each person of the Godhead should be as distinct as that person's involvement within redemption. Clearly, there is room within the unity of God for one person exclusively to assume human nature, for two persons to receive prayers which the other does not, and for one person to be the object of another's expulsive wrath. There cannot suddenly be less 'room' when Trinitarian communion comes under consideration. There must be a correlation between the

---

12. Macleod, op. cit., 126.

two realms of salvation and devotion: to precisely the same degree that Christian salvation revolves around three sharply distinguishable selves, Christian devotion must do the same. I may relate to the Son (or, indeed, any other divine person) in a way that is every bit as idiosyncratic as the manner in which he contributed to my redemption.

Salvation Gives Communion Its Emphases

The main connection between distinct communion and salvation has now been established: salvation, floodlighting as it does an irreducibly tri-personal God, justifies the practice of distinct communion. That is a crucial conclusion to have reached. But it may now be extended in one important way. For salvation does not only justify distinct communion; it also informs and shapes it. It provides the emphases on which communion with the different persons fastens. It furnishes the believer with relevant 'subject matter' for each strand of the three-way devotional relationship.

Owen refers scathingly to 'that way of praying to the Trinity, by the repetition of the same petition to the several persons.'[13] Though ostensibly respecting the tri-personal shape of communion (for Father, Son and Spirit are all addressed), this kind of prayer ends up blurring the persons' distinctness after all: the Father may as well be the Son, and the Son the Spirit, if they are related to in identical ways. Instead, then, the believer's relationship with each person should have its own thematic focal points, and these may be derived from the salvation storyline. Owen presses the point in this delightful paragraph:

---

13. John Owen, *Of Communion with God the Father, Son, and Holy Ghost, Each Person Distinctly, in Love, Grace, and Consolation* (1657), in *The Works of John Owen*, ed. William H. Goold (Edinburgh: Banner of Truth, 2004), 2:268.

There were [in the accomplishment of redemption] many acts of the will of the Father towards the Son — in sending, giving, appointing of him; in preparing him a body; in comforting and supporting him; in rewarding and giving a people unto him ... And in these things is the person of the Father in the divine being proposed unto us to be known and adored ... The Son condescendeth, consenteth, and engageth to do and accomplish in his own person the whole work which ... was appointed for him ... And in these divine operations is the person of the Son revealed unto us to be honoured ...[14]

Owen is not content that each person be 'known and adored' by the believer *as a distinct person*. That is only the starting point for tri-personal communion. In its full-blown form, each person is known and adored *in relation to his peculiar saving activities*. Communion with the Father focuses on his redemptive acts on our behalf, communion with the Son on his, and communion with the Spirit on his. That is the kind of Trinitarian devotion which Owen desires to promote.

The importance of this insight cannot be overestimated. It is the bridge between *being theoretically sympathetic toward distinct communion* and *being able to practise it with vitality*. A believer may sense the appropriateness of relating distinctly to the divine persons and yet, when actually on her knees before the triune God, feel directionless. Here, however, direction is provided. When Owen's approach is employed, Trinitarian devotion ceases to be amorphous and becomes orderly. The different roles performed within the gospel supply the different foci for person-specific prayers and songs. It is beautiful and animating to have meaningfully particular things to say to the Father and to the Son and to the Spirit — things that relate to their particular

14. Owen, *Works*, 3:158-59.

areas of redeeming activity. As Macleod puts it (discussing communion with Christ, specifically): 'It is...in terms of his peculiar role in redemption...that the Son's unique personality is defined for Christian faith and experience.'[15]

'Unique personality' is in short supply when he is contemplated merely as the eternal Son; then the bare title is all that really distinguishes him from the other two persons. It is not easy to relate distinctly to someone who is so undefined. But relating to him as the incarnate, crucified and risen redeemer is altogether different. Then we offer adoration that could only be his; words of devotion that could not be 'copied and pasted' into our interactions with the Spirit or the Father. We sing:

> I love thee because thou hast first loved me
> and purchased my pardon on Calvary's tree;
> I love thee for wearing the thorns on thy brow;
> if ever I loved thee, my Jesus, 'tis now.[16]

Artificiality?

But in order to be fully enjoyed, this stress on knowing and adoring the persons according to their saving exploits must also be defended. It must be defended, first, against the charge of artificiality. We know from ordinary human life that in any intimate relationship authenticity is necessary. It may be possible in the public domain to present ourselves in a way that bears little relation to who we really are. But within our marriages or close friendships that will not do. For those deep relationships to work, we must be willing to reveal our true selves.

---

15. Macleod, op. cit., 138.

16. From the hymn, 'My Jesus, I Love Thee,' by William Ralph Featherston (1842-70).

It is not otherwise with the divine persons. If we are to have genuine communion with them, we must engage with each person in his truest form. But Owen's approach may appear inimical to that. He wishes us to know and adore these *eternal* persons according to their *temporal* saving activities. Is that adequate? With the Father, the Son and the Spirit, is there not in each case a sharp divide between *person* and *work*? And in our Christian devotion should we not seek to plumb the depths of the former rather than paddle in the shallows of the latter?

But such concerns betray an underlying assumption. They assume that the redemptive roles adopted by Father, Son and Spirit bear a loose and arbitrary relationship to the persons' eternal identities. If that were true, then Christian devotion would indeed have to probe beyond those redemptive roles. It would be in the deeper realities of his being — not in, for instance, his sending of the Son — that (to use those words of Owen) 'the person of the Father…[is] to be known and adored.' If his saving work were a throwaway add-on to his essential self, then, indeed, it should not be our ultimate point of interest. The Father of the gospel story would be a mere artificial persona. To the Father himself, pure and stripped of all associations with the created realm, the communing soul would need somehow to penetrate.

The assumption, however, is wrong. The persons' redemptive roles are *not* arbitrary. As we argued in the previous chapter, when God acts, he does so in a way that befits his ontology. His external works cannot be disingenuous. They cannot tell us things about God that are not true. That would be a stain on his character, an undermining of his faithfulness. 'It is axiomatic for the integrity of theology that God is as he reveals himself to be.'[17] Of course, God was not

17. Sinclair B. Ferguson, *The Holy Spirit* (Downers Grove,

obliged to save (or, indeed, to create anything in the first place). He freely chooses to do so. His saving activity does not, therefore, belong to his essential being; he is complete whether or not he saves. But while not *belonging to* his essential being, his saving activity, once freely chosen, must *reflect* it. If God saves as three highly distinct persons, those distinctions must be traceable to an eternal reality — that was the point established in chapter four. And the point being made now is that if those persons adopt particular roles as they save, those roles, too, must be traceable to an eternal reality.

Owen affirms this in a dense but significant sentence:

> On those divine works which outwardly are of God there is an especial impression ... of the operation of each person, with respect unto their natural and necessary subsistence, as also with regard unto their internal characteristical properties, whereby we are distinctly taught to know them and adore them.[18]

Indelibly impressed on the persons' outward operations, Owen insists, are their 'internal characteristical properties'. *Person* and *work* cannot be divorced. The Son's incarnation and sin-bearing are not simply activities for which he happened to volunteer himself on the basis that someone had to do them! They are at a deep, ontological level Son-

---

Illinois: Inter-Varsity Press, 1996), 76.

18. Owen, *Works*, 3:95. Karl Rahner displays an affinity with Owen on this point when he complains: 'Starting from Augustine ... it has been among theologians a more or less foregone conclusion that each of the divine persons ... could have become man, so that the incarnation of precisely this person can tell us nothing about the peculiar features of *this* person within the divinity' (Karl Rahner, *The Trinity* [London: Burns and Oates, 1970], 11).

like activities. They could not have been assigned to another. To commune with the Son while focusing attention on his incarnation and sin-bearing is therefore to commune with the *real* Son. And the same could be said of communing with the Father while focusing attention on his work, or communing with the Spirit while focusing attention on his. In each case the person himself is truly being known and adored. Actual, authentic engagement with these eternal members of the Godhead is taking place. The charge of artificiality is not sustainable.[19]

Idolatry?

However, this notion of focusing our communion with the persons upon their saving roles faces a further challenge. It is a challenge which comes into play when communion with the Son is under consideration. His saving role, as we have already discussed in this chapter, involves incarnation. Therefore, to adore the Son as the Son of the gospel drama is to adore a man. He is not, of course, *only* a man; but a man he truly is. Yet no man ought to be adored. It is idolatrous to

---

19. These considerations seem to me to question the helpfulness of the common distinction between *person* and *work*. The distinction may serve a purpose in the ordering of a classical Christology or Pneumatology: it is reasonable first to establish Christ's deity, for example, or the Spirit's personhood, before moving on to redemptive roles. In the realm of Christian piety, however, I am less persuaded of its benefits. Those with responsibilities for leading worship services, for instance, should not feel that it is improper and a touch man-centred to jump straight into those things that have been done for us in the gospel — as though that ought to be deferred until the triune God has first been contemplated simply for who he is. Such rigid prioritising of *person* over *work* does not represent a more reverent and theocentric approach to worship. It is rather a failure to appreciate that to encounter Father, Son and Spirit in the act of redeeming sinners is to encounter them at their truest.

worship that which is created, and humanness by definition is created. The Son's humanness was a creation of the Spirit in the virgin's womb. Surely, then, for this reason if no other, Christian devotion must drill deeper than the persons' saving roles. It must engage with Father, Son and Spirit as they are outside of the gospel drama. In the case of the Son at least, that alone is safe. To revere him simply as the eternal Son is orthodox, uncompromised worship. To revere him as the Son made flesh, on the other hand, is to risk infringing the second commandment.

Such an objection may appear plausible. It ought, however, to be rejected. The form of communion we are commending is no more susceptible to the charge of idolatry than it is to the charge of artificiality. An adequate answer was formulated long ago in terms of an important distinction. The seventeenth-century theologian, Francis Cheynell, is a notable champion of this distinction. Vexed at the Lutheran justification for worshipping the incarnate Son — 'They say, that the Divine Majesty, Worship, Glory, Omnipotence, Omnipresence of the Son of God are communicated to Christ *as man*'[20] — Cheynell instead defended the practice in this way:

> The Material Object of worship is Christ, who is both God and man, the Son of David, the Son of Mary…the Mediator and Saviour of his people from their sins. The Formal Object…[is] the Coessential and Eternal Son of God, who is one and the same God with the Father and the Holy Spirit.[21]

The distinction, then, is between the *objectum formale* and the *objectum materiale* in the worship of the Son. More

20. Francis Cheynell, *The Divine Trinunity of the Father, Son, and Holy Spirit* (London: T.R & E.M. for Samuel Gellibrand, 1650), 332-33.
21. Ibid., 338-39.

colloquially, it is between the *why* and the *who*. *Why* is the Son worshipped? Solely because he is a divine person. *Who* is this Son to whom worship is offered? He is a divine person who assumed human nature and died for our sins on Golgotha's cross. The *why* preserves the worship from idolatry. The believer's communion with the Son may focus on the Good Friday event without any deification of the flesh there pierced with nails; and on Bethlehem's natal scene without any divinising of the infantile human mind there unable to express itself in words. The communion fastens on the Son's redeeming actions as its *subject matter* but rests on his underlying deity as its *warrant*. It is thus absolved of any suggestion of being profane.[22]

A Distinctive Garb

Redemption, then, does not simply reveal three distinct persons who ought to be engaged with distinctly. It also provides us with the *content* of that distinct engagement. It clothes each person in a distinctive garb which dictates how we relate to him. For the redemption-focused believer, the Godhead does not comprise Person A, Person B and Person C, amongst whom easily interchangeable expressions of devotion are randomly allocated. It does not even comprise Father, Son and Spirit, merely. Rather, there is the Father who chose us and sent his Son for us; there is the Son who took our flesh, suffered vicariously and conquered death; and there is the Spirit who empowered Jesus and empowers us. *Those* are

---

22. Cf. the felicitous words of James Durham: 'A soul may pray to Jesus, who died, who made satisfaction, who intercedes, &c. and, upon that consideration, be affected with love, strengthened in hope and confidence in its prayer, which yet is put up to him, because he is God' (James Durham, *A Learned and Complete Commentary upon the Book of Revelation, Delivered in Several Lectures* [Glasgow: David Niven, 1788], 30.

the three with whom we commune. We commune with each as none other than that redeeming agent. And we discover that such communion is marvellously inexhaustible. In their saving actions on our behalf resides endless material for person-specific devotion. Throughout eternal ages, indeed, that well will not run dry!

PART 3

THE PRACTICAL OUTWORKING
OF DISTINCT COMMUNION

CHAPTER SIX

The Joy of Tri-Personal Devotion

The foregoing chapters of this book have made a case for distinct communion. The practice, it has been argued, is warranted. It is warranted *exegetically*: the New Testament uses communion language and imagery in an indiscriminately tri-personal way. And it is warranted *theologically*: biblical soteriology displays a God whose personal distinctions are sufficiently pronounced as to invite distinguishable relationships with Father, Son and Spirit.

But notice carefully that sentence in the preceding paragraph: 'The *practice* is warranted.' For when it comes to distinct communion, 'practice' is the operative word. Of course, defending and propounding it as a *concept* has its place; but, sooner or later, it must actually be *done*! Communion with the triune God belongs, ultimately, not in a book like this, but in the Sunday church gathering and in the quiet bedroom where a solitary believer prays.

But when the attempt is made to move from the theoretical to the practical realm, and to engage distinctly with the three persons, questions and concerns inevitably arise. Thus, in the last part of this book we shall turn to the implementation of distinct communion — its actual execution by the believing individual or congregation. And in this chapter we shall do so deriving helpful stimuli from two sources.

The first is the Scottish seventeenth-century theologian, James Durham. Durham's voluminous commentary on the Book of Revelation, published in 1658, comprises a series of lectures. The first of these bears the title, 'Concerning the Holy Trinity and Object of Worship,' and, following an initial defence of the doctrine of the Trinity itself, becomes a discussion of distinct communion. At points in the discussion, Durham appears to share Owen's bold stance. One paragraph, for instance, sees him insisting that 'the Holy Ghost may be expressly prayed unto, as the Father, and the Son'.[1] At the same time, however, a couple of Durham's emphases are calculated, in my view, to undermine full-blown tri-personal devotion. As these emphases relate closely to the area of *practice*, they are relevant to the purpose of this chapter. The process of respectfully disagreeing with Durham's practical considerations will, hopefully, prove useful. It will clarify our approach as we seek to be better doers of distinct communion.

Our other stimulus will be the pulpit prayers of Charles Spurgeon. Like his sermons, many of Spurgeon's public prayers were transcribed and are extant. In this case we shall profit not by disagreeing, but by simply admiring. The prayers of this nineteenth-century preacher contain

---

1. James Durham, *A Learned and Complete Commentary upon the Book of Revelation, Delivered in Several Lectures* (Glasgow: David Niven, 1788), 25. Intriguingly, he appears to think that prayers to the Spirit have Scriptural precedents: 'Where [biblical] petitions do especially respect the increase of grace, which is the work of the Spirit, we...find him expressly mentioned' (ibid., 25-26). The matter of praying to the Spirit is addressed in the final chapter of this book.

the finest examples of distinct communion that I have encountered anywhere.

Objectum Considerationis

We shall begin, then, with Durham. Central to his treatment of worship in the aforementioned lecture is a threefold distinction. Two parts of it we have encountered already. In chapter five we discussed briefly the *objectum formale* and the *objectum materiale*: the former refers to the basis of or reason for worship; the latter to its actual recipient. In approaching the Son, we observed, it is his deity alone that warrants the worship (*objectum formale*), but it is the incarnate redeemer whom we actually adore (*objectum materiale*). Durham, however, makes much of a third principle: the *objectum considerationis*. This, he says, is:

> The consideration that the worshipper hath of [the] object in worshipping of him; and is as a motive thereto, or is (as the learned Voetius calls it, *Specificatio Objecti*) the specification of the object, whereby the heart of the worshipper, by taking up the object worshipped under such a consideration, is warmed with love and thankfulness, and strengthened in his confidence, to worship that object.[2]

Durham, as mentioned above, is favourably disposed toward the concept of distinct communion. But he views it through the lens of this principle, the *objectum considerationis*. Prayers addressed to particular persons serve to highlight the saving actions for which those persons are responsible; and the highlighting of those saving actions moves the worshipper to pray more believingly and more fervently. He focuses, as an example, on praying to Christ:

---

2. Ibid., 28

As any of the persons may be named in prayer; so, *for strengthening of our faith*, may the Mediator be named and prayed unto under such titles and relations as agree only to him, and not to any other person.[3]

Later, he focuses more specifically on praying to Christ as our heavenly intercessor. He envisages the believer exclaiming, 'O Advocate, plead for me.' This, he says, is a valuable way of praying, provided that:

there be a right up-taking of [Christ's] intercession, that in the time while he … is prayed unto, faith be exercised on the virtue of his intercession …; so, that expression [i.e. designating Christ as the object of the prayer] is but made use of *for strengthening of faith*.[4]

Of course, the strengthening of faith is always desirable. If, however, that is all that is at stake here, then distinct communion is not such a pressing matter after all. It scarcely merits the writing of *this* book, let alone Owen's weighty tome! At the end of his comments on praying to Christ as advocate, Durham airily remarks, 'It must be one in the matter, as if, in different expressions, by naming the Father, we should pray, *O Father, make me partaker of all the benefits of Christ's intercession*'.[5] And perhaps nowhere is his tone more dismissive regarding these variations in prayer than when he writes:

When there is an alteration of the expression … it is the continued worshipping of the same object, GOD, however he be designed: or, whatever be the expressions … which we seek to strengthen our faith by.[6]

---

3. Ibid., 31 (italics mine).
4. Ibid., 31 (italics mine).
5. Ibid., 31.
6. Ibid., 31.

The issue, then, which Durham's excursus throws into relief is this: is there any *objective* preferableness about the practice of distinct communion, or are its benefits purely *subjective*? Are we in fact worshipping God no differently whatever the verbal addressee — whether 'Father,' 'Son,' 'Spirit' or 'my Trinity' — because these are mere 'expressions' (to use one of Durham's recurring terms), and of considerably less importance than God's indivisible oneness? These are intensely practical questions: the believer needs to know whether distinct communion is an urgent priority because of its intrinsic value, or merely a useful devotional aid. Several responses may be made.

First, although the concerns which have prompted the writing of this book might incline me to do so, I am wary of reacting too dogmatically to Durham. He focuses on the potential of distinct communion to strengthen faith; it is tempting to veer right away from that subjective approach and insist instead on distinct communion as the only truly God-honouring option! But that would not be right. When the validity of Christian devotion depends upon its conformity to a set of procedures, it ceases to be devotion. We have then descended into ritualism; communion with God has become an art form which the believer tries to 'get right'. Durham, indeed, is to be commended when he writes:

> We grant, that sometimes, *de facto*, [a divine name or title] may be used in sincerity, and accepted by God, when there is much confusion in reference to ... the person: because it may have what is essential, viz. an adoring of God, and an exercise of faith in Christ, under that expression ... Thus, no question, many prayers of the saints, where faith hath been in the Mediator, have been accepted, although there hath been much indistinctness, as to the object, in many things.[7]

---

7. Ibid., 31-32.

Prayer is not formulaic. Devotional authenticity is never to be equated with addressing particular divine persons at particular points. The believer whose Christian faith is Trinitarian, but who spends a lifetime addressing only the Father, say, in prayer, is not thereby a stranger to genuine communion with God.

Moreover, Durham is correct that Christ's role as intercessor does not mean that he has to be the person addressed whenever his intercession is contemplated. The prayer, 'O Father, make me partaker of all the benefits of Christ's intercession,' is, indeed, a legitimate one. In Ephesians 1:17 Paul prays for an imparting to the Ephesian believers of the Spirit's wisdom and revelation; but the prayer is addressed to the Father, not to the Spirit himself. Jesus, similarly, refers to the Holy Spirit being given to those who ask (Luke 11:13); but the one asked is the Father rather than the Spirit himself. These biblical instances remind us that distinct communion must not become rigid. It is natural, as we discussed in the previous chapter, to speak to each person about those redemptive areas with which he has a closer connection than the other persons. But no divine person has a monopoly on any area of redemption. No aspect of my salvation is inapplicable and off-limits because I happen to be addressing the Son, for instance, rather than the Spirit or the Father.

Secondly, however, the concessions just made do not mean that distinct communion is little more than an esoteric luxury. A particular way of approaching God may be valid (because God is gracious and accommodating towards his people); but it may also contain much room for improvement, much room to be made more God-honouring.[8] For surely

---

8. Paul appears to sanction a distinction between *a worship practice that is valid* and *a worship practice that is optimal* when he

God is most honoured by that form of communion which takes most seriously his self-disclosure in Scripture — that form of communion which corresponds most closely to who he is. Such communion (in an overall sense throughout the Christian life, not in its every individual act) will blend a number of elements: it will sometimes approach the three together, crying 'My Trinity' — for that reflects the oneness of God; it will sometimes focus protractedly on one person, thanking and praising him for *all* aspects of salvation — for that reflects God's non-compartmentalised way of operating; and it will often focus successively on the three, thanking and praising each for *particular* aspects of salvation — for that reflects God's irreducible tripersonality. Communion which falls short of these contours suffers from an *objective* deficiency. It is not just that a helpful motivational tool is being squandered; the communion itself is poorer than it might be. It does not align satisfactorily with the being upon whom it is focused, the being for whom it exists.

Thirdly, the argument which makes distinct communion objectively unnecessary could in fact do the same for Trinitarian belief itself. If, as Durham appears to suggest, Christian devotion rises to the one God however I address him, then might the same be true however I conceive of him? If I can exclude two divine persons, say, from my prayers (because, God being one, those persons are not different objects of worship from the person I do include), can I also exclude them from my very understanding of the God to whom I pray? It is dangerous when the 'one indivisible

---

writes, 'Earnestly desire to prophesy, and do not forbid speaking in tongues' (1 Cor. 14:39). It is my understanding that prophesying and speaking in tongues were both, during the apostolic era, channels of divine communication to his people. Clearly, however, Paul does not regard them equally: one he glowingly commends; the other he does not commend but cannot condemn.

Godhead"[9] is so emphasised that it barely continues to matter which person(s) one is dealing with; when the single divine essence shines through each person so overwhelmingly that it alone can be seen. It is the onset of modalism, the denial of proper personhood to the three.

In that connection I shall quote Durham at length as he summarises the cardinal principles of Christian worship:

> Having these following things fixed in our hearts by faith, (which we conceive more simply necessary to worship, whatever the expressions be) viz. 1. An impression of the holiness, justice, omnisciency, and glory of God, &c. and

---

9. Durham, *Revelation*, 27. Of course, the 'one indivisible Godhead' *does* mean that the same God is worshipped whichever person is named. Owen also makes that point: 'The divine nature is the reason and cause of all worship; so that it is impossible to worship any one person, and not worship the whole Trinity' (John Owen, *Of Communion with God the Father, Son, and Holy Ghost, Each Person Distinctly, in Love, Grace, and Consolation* [1657], in *The Works of John Owen*, ed. William H. Goold [Edinburgh: Banner of Truth, 2004], 2:268). But that truth does not diminish the importance and necessity of distinct communion for Owen as it appears to do for Durham. For the Englishman, indeed, it amounts to little more than a footnote in a tome whose overwhelming concern is that 'the saints have distinct communion with the Father, and the Son, and the Holy Spirit' (Ibid., 2:9).

Thomas Goodwin, moreover, expressly rejects using God's indivisibility as a reason for 'stinting' oneself when it comes to distinct communion. He calls for a 'labouring after a distinct knowing of, and communion with all three persons. ...not only...to have fellowship with the one in the other implicitly, but distinctly with the one and with the other, and distinctly with the one as with the other' (Thomas Goodwin, *The Object and Acts of Justifying Faith*, in *The Works of Thomas Goodwin* [Edinburgh: James Nichol, 1865], 8:377). 'Implicitly' is the key word, there. In the last analysis Durham appears to be content with the implicit worship of all the persons, whichever is/are actually contemplated and addressed; Goodwin, like Owen, is not.

THE JOY OF TRI-PERSONAL DEVOTION

suitable affections with the present work, viz. such as the worshipping of such a God doth call for. 2. A conviction that we are praying to that one glorious God, whatever our expressions be; that it is he we are worshipping; that it is our duty to adore him; and that it is from him that we expect what we pray for, whatever the designation in the petition be, and whatever person be named. 3. An impression of our own sinful disproportionableness to that work, and of the utter incapacity that we stand in of having access to God, or any ground of expecting any thing from him, in respect of ourselves, if it be not obtained by virtue of Christ Jesus his satisfaction and intercession. 4. An exercising of faith on Christ the Mediator, for attaining of what is prayed for, from God, by the mediation of the Mediator. All which are necessary, and where they are, we conceive, the soul is to silence all other questionings, and to hold here.[10]

Of course, Durham's second point there is the most pertinent — once again displaying a cool indifference to 'expressions,' 'designations,' and the *naming of persons* in prayer. But no less striking is the general absence of Trinitarianism throughout this summary of the principles Christian worshippers should have 'fixed in [their] hearts'. In one sense, given the title of Durham's lecture and its opening, robust assertion of the Trinity,[11] it is a staggering place for him to end up. In another sense it is unsurprising: the same tendency which devalues distinct communion will, ultimately, corrode Trinitarian religion more broadly.

To return, then, to the practical question here: should every believer be urgently interested in distinct communion?

---

10. Ibid., 33.
11. This sentence captures the tone of the first few pages: 'This truth concerning the blessed and glorious Trinity...coming so near to the nature of God himself, it cannot but be exceedingly necessary for Christians to be thorough in the faith thereof' (ibid., 24).

Durham's treatment yields an uncertain answer, which we might paraphrase as follows: *The three persons in their distinctness are an attractive objectum considerationis calculated to broaden the worshipper's panorama of salvation, as the Father's election and the Son's mission and the Spirit's indwelling all come endearingly into view.* That is as far as Durham will go. In my view it is not nearly far enough. Distinct communion presses a stronger claim on the Christian worshipper than that. Its merits are more than merely subjective. This practice is the axiomatic response to the revelation God has given of himself; it honours the being who exists and saves us as Father, Son and Spirit. It is Trinitarian religion come into its own, the death knell of wretched modalism. It is the richest form of Christian devotion. Every believer should aspire to it. As Goodwin writes, concluding his extraordinary plea for distinct communion, 'We should never be satisfied till we have attained it.'[12]

Transitions Within Prayer

It was mentioned at the beginning of the chapter that a couple of Durham's emphases are calculated to undermine full-blown tri-personal devotion. One of those, the *objectum considerationis*, we have now discussed. The other is a particular aversion which he expresses more than once in the lecture. Durham dislikes Trinitarian transitions within a single prayer: the movement from addressing one divine person to addressing another. The reason for this aversion is (again) the indivisibility of the Godhead, allied to the weakness of our minds. By itself the indivisibility of the Godhead would not exclude these transitions. The problem is that our weak minds, when shifting between the persons

---

12. Goodwin, *Works*, 8:379.

in prayer, may lose sight of God's indivisibility. They may gravitate in a tritheistic direction.

This is how he articulates his concern in one place:

> By naming one person after he hath named another, (suppose he name the Father at first, and afterward the Son) he doth not vary the object of worship, as if he were praying to another than formerly; but...still it is the same one God. Because our imagination is ready to foster such divided conceptions, we conceive, it is safest not to alter the denomination of the persons in the same prayer.[13]

In another place he speaks in these off-putting terms of shifting between the persons:

> We conceive ... that change should be warily used, lest it breed ... any such thoughts [i.e. of a divided God] ... the generality of people being prone to imagine different objects of worship in such cases.[14]

Durham appears to have uppermost in his mind those whose role it is to lead congregational worship ('especially, where it is in the hearing of others, who possibly may have such thoughts, though we have none').[15] But whether it is public intercession or private, one thing is clear: he harbours grave misgivings about mid-prayer transitions.

Once again, several responses are in order. First, Durham's criterion — what is 'safest' — could just as effectively support the opposite conclusion regarding transitions. It could be argued that naming only one person in a prayer might breed in weak minds a unipersonal conception of God; therefore, it is safest to move between the persons. For Durham,

---

13. Durham, *Revelation*, 28.
14. Ibid., 31.
15. Ibid., 28.

however, safety only appears to apply in one direction: it means preserving God's unity at all costs, but not God's tri-personality. A thoroughgoing Trinitarian theology ought to be no less concerned with the latter than with the former.

Actually, in raising safety concerns about omitting transitions from our prayers, I am not being facetious. For the evangelical church of the twenty-first century, the threat to Trinitarianism does not come, largely, from heretical theologians and heterodox schools of thought. It comes, rather, from vagueness and imprecision in the way that Christianity is practised. As was mentioned in the introduction to this book, many public prayers are punctuated by the simple vocative, 'Lord.' It is possible that those who voice such prayers — as well as those who hear them and give their 'amen' — do so with the Lord Jesus in mind; or that they use the title thinking of the one Lord who is Father, Son and Spirit. In such cases all is well: those are healthy notions, congenial to the truth that God is persons. But it is equally possible that no one in the room has any clear idea of what is meant by the repeated 'Lord;' and that the notion of a plurality of divine persons is wholly absent from every worshipper's mind. One suspects that may often be the case. And it is alarming. In this manner a de facto Unitarianism can take hold of orthodox churches without a single item of their creeds being altered. In such a climate, public prayers which move between the divine persons may in fact be the great need of the hour. Rather than being the recipe for tritheism which Durham feared, such prayers might just be a useful check to the contemporary trend to see God as unipersonal.

Secondly, if the shifting of focus from one person to another is unsafe, why confine the danger to the realm of prayer? Ought not the Apostles' Creed, for instance, to come under suspicion? In reciting it the worshipper moves with some rapidity from Father to Son to Spirit. Can we cope with that if we have such a tendency 'to imagine different objects of worship'? Should all our liturgies be risk-assessed, and every acknowledgement of the different divine persons made thoroughly confusion-proof?

It seems to me that the real issue here is this: should Christian worship be dictated by the capacities of our minds, or by the realities of God's being? In *Mere Christianity* C.S. Lewis concedes that Trinitarian religion is a delicate business, full of pitfalls for the careless worshipper. But he concludes his chapter on 'The Three-Personal God' in this helpful way:

> If Christianity was something we were making up, of course we could make it easier. But it is not. We cannot compete, in simplicity, with people who are inventing religions. How could we? We are dealing with Fact. Of course anyone can be simple if he has no facts to bother about.[16]

If God has revealed himself to be three irreducibly distinct persons existing in interpenetrative unity, it is our responsibility to worship accordingly — whatever the dangers involved. Worshipping the real God, who transcends our powers of comprehension, *is* risky. When we try to make it safer, we may in fact be attempting to make God himself safer.

Thirdly, it is arguable that a proper enjoyment of God's triune nature ought to manifest itself in a kind of oscillation when praying. We used that term in a previous chapter in relation to the divine *he-ness* and the divine *they-ness*. We established that there is a healthy oscillation between those

16. C.S. Lewis, *Mere Christianity* (Glasgow: Collins, 1956), 140-41.

two realities which the praying believer can experience — as expressed so thrillingly by Gregory Nazianzen: 'No sooner do I conceive of the One than I am illumined by the Splendour of the Three; no sooner do I distinguish Them than I am carried back to the One.'[17] Gregory cannot get enough of either dimension of God's being: he rushes from the one to the three, and back again, like a wonder-filled child — pulled, magnetically, in both directions!

But in those moments when the worshipper is in distinguishing mode, and 'the splendour of the Three' (rather than the one) is overwhelming the mind, surely the magnetic pulls only proliferate. For then the communing soul is confronted with one divine person who alone affords an eternity of contemplation, and another divine person of whom exactly the same is true, and still another as well! Feeling with Samuel Rutherford, 'I know not which divine person I love the most, but...I need and love each of them,'[18] the enraptured believer must give in to the threefold magnetism, unable to remain focused on the Father for long without the Spirit coming into view as an equally suitable addressee; before, soon, the Son comes to the fore as a comparably worthy object of attention; and so it goes on, this constantly shifting devotional choreography.

The holy Trinity is beautiful, infinitely outstripping every other beauty that exists. This sublime, tri-personal God is to be enjoyed by believing hearts. And luxuriating fully in the glorious Trinity will entail, almost inevitably,

---

17. Gregory Nazianzen, *Orations* 40.41, in *The Nicene and Post-Nicene Fathers*, vol. 7, ed. Philip Schaff and Henry Wace (Grand Rapids, Michigan: Wm. B. Eerdmans Publishing Company, 1978), 375.

18. Quoted in Joel R. Beeke, *Puritan Reformed Spirituality* (Grand Rapids, Michigan: Reformation Heritage Books, 2004), 435.

an oscillating kind of communion: as the undivided *he* and the irreducible *they* alternately enthral; and as the unique lustres of Father, Son and Spirit successively catch the eye. It is this note of irrepressible delight that seems to be missing in Durham's anxious aversion to mid-prayer transitions. Brian Kay comments that 'the trinitarian character of Christian devotion should be so deeply rooted as to manifest itself spontaneously in different degrees of complexity.'[19] Durham, however, appears to fear spontaneity in Trinitarian devotion, and permits only one degree of complexity: the addressing of a single divine person in each individual prayer.

Fourthly, Durham's concerns ought not to be met with abstract arguments alone. Our evangelical heritage supplies us with concrete expressions of hypostatically nuanced prayers which, in some cases at least, may prove more compelling than Durham's objections. That in fact is the cue for Durham to take his leave of our discussions, and for our other 'stimulus' now to take centre stage.

The Pulpit Prayers of Charles Spurgeon

Charles Spurgeon, leading his congregation in prayer during Sunday services, frequently made seamless transitions between the divine persons. And this was not the crass habit of a doctrinally lightweight pulpiteer! In one of his sermons, he exhorts his congregation:

> Magnify Father, Son, and Holy Spirit. Shun that ministry which dishonours either of these blessed persons and seek to be fully built up and instructed in the Gospel teaching which glorifies Father, Son, and Spirit in divine equality, and leads your own hearts into "the grace of our Lord Jesus

---

19. Brian Kay, *Trinitarian Spirituality: John Owen and the Doctrine of God in Western Devotion* (Milton Keynes: Paternoster, 2007), 33.

Christ, the love of God the Father, and the communion of the Holy Ghost."[20]

Words like these supply the backdrop to Spurgeon's distinctive form of Trinitarian praying. The kind of ministry which he here urges his congregation to prize was presumably the kind of ministry to which he himself also aspired: a ministry that glorified Father, Son, and Spirit and led his congregation's hearts into an experience of them all. Thus, Spurgeon's penchant for fluid public prayers — in which the specific addressee could change at several points — was entirely in keeping with these first principles of his ministry.

Prayer is special and sacred. One hesitates to analyse too scientifically words which have been offered devotionally to God. It does not seem entirely appropriate to subject them to scrutiny. However, the pervasive Trinitarianism in Spurgeon's prayers is too rare and important to be left unexamined. A few observations, hopefully, will not violate these 'sacrifices of praise' (Heb. 13:15), but will serve to magnify the distinct communion which, in my opinion, is no small part of their beauty. Two features of that distinct communion are striking.

Variety

In every way Spurgeon's pulpit prayers exude variety. This is no mean feat — as any man who regularly leads congregational worship is painfully aware! Most conspicuously, their *themes* are varied. Spurgeon's prayers adore God, thank God, petition God and confess sins to God. They make reference to creation, providence, redemption, judgement and the world to come. They quote from or allude to many different parts

---

20. From a sermon on Isaiah 53:11 (https://ccel.org/ccel/spurgeon/sermons61/sermons61.xxvi.html).

of the Bible. This impressive thematic range is the obvious form of variety encountered in the prayers.[21] But it is not the only form. The way that the prayers engage with the three divine persons also exhibits variety.

Indeed, before we even come to the distinct communion which they so often display, we should note that Spurgeon's Trinitarian prayers do not always take that form. Sometimes he engages with the three together as a single addressee. We commented earlier on the vocative 'Lord,' so prevalent today, and on the possibility of vague conceptions accompanying it. Spurgeon, too, uses that vocative, but in his case it is often clear that he has a concrete meaning in mind. And, frequently, that concrete meaning is *Father, Son and Spirit.* One of the prayers has the line, 'O Lord, we worship with all our heart.' Many of our contemporary prayers might leave that as a self-contained statement, as though it sufficiently clarifies the worship's intended recipient. Spurgeon, however, immediately continues, 'and adore the Father, the Son, and the Holy Ghost'.[22] Similarly, the petition, 'Oh Lord, teach us this very morning the art of praise,' is given more specific content in the next sentence: 'Let our soul…send forth a delicious perfume of praiseful gratitude unto the ever blessed One, Father, Son, and Holy Spirit.'[23] In another prayer the exclamation 'All our hearts worship Thee, Oh, Thou glorious Lord!' is immediately *preceded by* a fuller description of the addressee: 'Father, Son, and Spirit. The Triune God of Israel,

---

21. According to Peter Morden, it was precisely so that he could monitor his thematic range that Spurgeon had people transcribing his prayers each week (Peter J. Morden, 'C. H. Spurgeon and Prayer,' *Evangelical Quarterly* 84.4 [2012]: 326).

22. C.H. Spurgeon, *The Pastor in Prayer: Being a Choice Selection of C.H. Spurgeon's Sunday Morning Prayers* (Pasadena, Texas: Pilgrim Publications, 1971), 'King and Priest,' 80.

23. Ibid., 'The Sentence of Death in Ourselves,' 128.

we express most solemnly the reverence we feel for Thee; and render to Thee our humble adoration'.[24] In these instances, then, 'Lord' refers to the one Lord who is Father, Son and Spirit. Spurgeon is addressing the three in their *he-ness*, to use our earlier language. He is praying with a fully developed Trinitarian consciousness, but he is not directing distinct prayers to the distinct persons. His highly varied way of praying means he does not always approach the triune God practising distinct communion.

When, however, he does practise distinct communion, then the variety really springs to life. In one prayer entitled 'The Adorable Trinity' he moves from Father to Son to Spirit, devoting several sentences to each. The transitions in this prayer — though they would presumably have attracted James Durham's disapproval a couple of centuries earlier — are measured and sedate. In other prayers, however, they are quite different: in a breathless manner each divine person is addressed in turn within just three sentences. This is a typical example:

> O dear Saviour, there is room for the greatest faith to be exercised upon Thy blessed person and work. O God, the Most High and All-sufficient, there is room for the greatest confidence in Thee. O Divine Paraclete, the Holy Ghost, there is now sufficient room for the fullest faith in Thine operations.[25]

Here is another:

> We now commit ourselves again to Thy keeping, O faithful Creator; to Thy keeping, O Saviour of the pierced hand; to

24. Ibid., 'True Prayer — Heart Prayer,' 54-55.
25. Ibid., 'The Personal Touch,' 9. As is the case in many Trinitarian New Testament passages, 'God,' here, clearly means *the Father*.

Thy keeping, O eternal Spirit, who art able to keep us from falling, and to sanctify us wholly that we may be made to stand among the saints in light.[26]

One can only imagine Durham's reaction to prayers like these! Surely, however, they exemplify that magnetism discussed earlier in the chapter: lost in wonder, love and praise, Spurgeon is pulled from one infinitely desirable divine person to another.

But the variety extends further than this. It is not simply that in some cases Spurgeon devotes a few sentences to each person, and in other cases a single sentence to each. There are prayers in which his transitions are quite erratic. A prayer may be almost entirely addressed to one particular person, and yet contain within it one or two sudden, fleeting petitions to another. One prayer, for example, is directed largely to the Father, often mentioning Christ but in the third person ('Thou hast revealed Thyself in Christ Jesus;' 'Our trust is stayed...in...the person of Thy dear Son;' 'Oh, that...souls may...cast themselves before Thy face, trusting in Jesus'). However, one sentence near the start briefly alters that trend ('most blessed Jesus, fulfil Thine office as Mediator, bring us now near to God by Thy precious blood'), as do a few lines near the end:

---

26. Ibid., 'Trust and Pray,' 76-77. Note that the two excerpts quoted in this paragraph, though similar in the rapidity of their transitions, do not mention the persons in the same order: in the first the order is Son, Father, Spirit; in the second, Father, Son, Spirit. This represents a further touch of variety in Spurgeon's distinct communion: he is not restricted to a particular hypostatic sequence. Gregory Nazianzen would approve: 'Speak of God with Paul ... who sometimes counts up the Three Persons, and that in varied order, not keeping the same order, but reckoning one and the same Person now first, now second, now third' (Gregory Nazianzen, *Orations* 34.15, 338).

We do know, great King, that whilst Thou has a special kingdom in Thy people, yet the Lord hath given Thee power over all flesh; and we pray this may be recognised, and we may see it. Thy kingdom come, O Jesus; may Thy kingdom come — Thy Father's kingdom.[27]

Another prayer similarly focuses mainly on the Father. When it comes to a section in which the conversions of unbelievers are requested, he is petitioned, 'Look in great mercy upon the many that may be here, who never have believed in Jesus;' and again, 'We ask that this very morning, while Jesus Christ is lifted up, many may look unto Him.' Quite unexpectedly between those two petitions, however, Christ ceases to be the theme of a conversation Spurgeon is having with the Father, and becomes instead the one directly addressed:

O Strong Son of God, Immortal Love — whom, though we have not seen Thy face, we do believe in, and rely upon — ride forth this morning with Thine arrows dipped in Thine own blood, and shoot them out amongst this audience, that the people may fall under them, wounded with the sense of sin, smitten even to self-despair with a consciousness of guilt: and oh, that they might get healing from the hands that wound them, may they get life from the hand that kills their hope. May they look to Thee, anointed of the Lord, ennobled in the highest heaven, who once received the sinner here below in Thine own Person, and who still receiveth sinners: oh, that they might come to Thee and live.[28]

In these prayers the transitions between the persons do not conform to any regular, balanced structure. Spurgeon, as we saw, can practise that kind of distinct communion: (either slowly or rapidly) moving from person to person in an orderly manner. But he is not at all averse to impulsive,

---

27. Ibid., 'The Reason Why Many Cannot Find Rest,' 41-46.
28. Ibid., 'The Life Look,' 97-101.

unpredictable forays, whereby he suspends the protracted invocation of one person in order to invoke, momentarily, a different person.

One prayer in the collection is particularly fascinating. It begins as a celebration of our adoption as sons and, naturally, focuses on the Father. Suddenly, however, the Spirit is addressed: 'O Spirit of God, help our infirmities.' But the shift does not last long and, with the Father reclaiming the spotlight, the prayer appears to resemble those just mentioned: an offering predominantly to one person, but with a temporary deviation. However, this prayer is not in fact the same. As it proceeds, not only is the Spirit addressed *again*, but a large section of the prayer becomes devoted exclusively to him. For a stretch of approximately three hundred words, Spurgeon engages consistently with this divine person, punctuating his intercession with such vocatives as 'Spirit of God,' 'Divine Spirit' and 'sweet Spirit'.[29] The result is a splendidly idiosyncratic prayer in which the distribution of petitions among the persons is daringly free-form. This manner of engaging with the Trinity is the opposite of formulaic. No one, however familiar with Spurgeon's ways, could possibly have predicted the direction that this prayer's distinct communion would take.

I do not wish to weary the reader with too many examples. But hopefully those already provided hint at the breadth of possibilities which Spurgeon brought to his Trinitarian praying. The point is important. Some may fear that distinct communion turns prayer into drudgery. Prayer, it may be felt, is an outpouring of the soul's devotion that ought not to be complicated by the necessity of moving between the different persons. Probably, a misrepresentation of the practice lurks behind such concerns: we noted in an earlier chapter

---

29. Ibid., 'Intercession for the Saints,' 121-26.

Owen's aversion to one form of it ('praying to the Trinity, by the repetition of the same petition to the several persons'[30]) that is indeed tiresome and otiose. But Spurgeon's prayers demonstrate that, when done properly, distinct communion does not remotely inhibit and encumber Christian devotion. Certainly, the practice involves a degree of mental effort, an awareness at every point of which divine person is being addressed: Spurgeon never clumsily thanks the Father for dying on the cross, or expresses a longing for the Spirit's Parousia at the end of the age! (And why should prayer *not* involve mental effort? Loving God is not just a matter of heart and soul: the whole *mind* is also to be engaged [Mark 12:30]). But there is not the least hint of drudgery as Spurgeon engages with the different persons. On the contrary, the most scintillating *variety* characterises his distinct communion. Throughout the extant transcriptions, his tri-personal praying passes through numerous fresh configurations. Gregory Nazianzen's lovely description of Paul's letters applies almost equally well to Spurgeon's pulpit prayers:

> Sometimes he mentions Three, sometimes Two or One … And sometimes he attributes the operation of God to the Spirit … and sometimes instead of the Spirit he brings in Christ; and at times he separates the Persons saying, 'One God, of whom are all things, and we in Him; and one Lord Jesus Christ, by whom are all things, and we by Him;' at other times he brings together the one Godhead, 'For of Him and through Him and in Him are all things.'[31]

Redemptive Focus

Spurgeon's prayers are full of God's redemptive activity. I mentioned in a previous chapter that a man leading public

---

30. John Owen, *Works*, 2:268.
31. Gregory Nazianzen, *Orations* 34.15, 338.

prayers can feel bound to a certain order. He may sense that it is somehow improper to rush into *God's works* without focusing first on *who God is in himself*. Spurgeon betrays no such qualms. Often his prayers gravitate immediately to salvation's storyline. One begins: 'Most glorious Lord God, it is marvellous in our eyes that Thou shouldst become incarnate, that Thy Son should take our flesh upon Him.'[32] Another opens in this way: 'Gracious God, we praise Thee with our whole hearts for the wondrous revelation of Thy love in Christ Jesus our Lord. We think every day of His passion.'[33] Still another reaches by the third sentence the niceties of the Easter event: 'Our hearts this morning... would look back to the conflicts of Calvary, and see how our Lord for ever there broke the dragon's head.'[34] This hastiness is, in my view, healthy. It demonstrates a confidence that redemption is revelatory. Prayer does not need to begin with a restricted purview, initially ignoring God's external works and attempting to pry instead into his ontology. To view God in his saving of sinners is to view God as he really is.

But if Spurgeon's prayers, generally, make much of redemption, it is true, also, of those prayers which feature distinct communion. We established in chapter five that at its best distinct communion is shaped by the persons' roles in redemption. We relate to each according to his particular contribution. It ought to be apparent from the excerpts already offered that this is exactly how Spurgeon proceeds. We have observed him calling upon Christ to perform the role of mediator, and requesting the Spirit to help his people's infirmities. Such petitions are not arbitrarily assigned. It is

---

32. C.H. Spurgeon, *The Pastor in Prayer*, 'Sitting Over Against the Sepulchre,' 37.

33. Ibid., 'Jesus Interceding for Transgressors,' 13.

34. Ibid., 'Your Adversary,' 109.

not on a whim that Spurgeon chooses either Father, Son or Spirit as the recipient of a particular prayer. Rather, he directs and distributes his petitions in a way that corresponds to the unique input of each person within salvation.

The clearest glimpses of this emerge when Spurgeon moves quickly between the persons. Here is one example:

> We adore Thee, O Father, for Thy great love in the gift of Jesus: we equally adore Thee, most blessed Jesus, for resigning Thy life for our sakes: and then we adore the Blessed Spirit who has led us to know this mystery and to put our trust in Jesus.[35]

In these lines Spurgeon focuses on the very core of each person's redeeming work — the Father's giving, the Son's dying and the Spirit's converting of sinners — as he adores the three. Another example, however, is slightly different: 'Jesus of Nazareth, pass by just now! Divine Spirit, rest upon us now! Holy Father, look upon Thy children now.'[36] Here, the activities associated with each person are not the core and obvious ones. However, although more obscure, they are still valid associations; they have not been plucked out of the air. The third petition is the most straightforward: it is indubitably a role of the Father to adopt us as his children and regard us with a paternal eye. The second petition seems to be based on 1 Peter 4:14, according to which the Spirit, usually said to indwell the believer, does indeed in another sense 'rest upon' her. The first petition appears to take its cue from Luke 18:35-43, where Jesus passes by a blind beggar and heals the man. In that moment from Christ's earthly ministry, Spurgeon presumably detects an adumbration of Christ's post-ascension, heavenly ministry: still, as his

---

35. Ibid., 'Jesus Interceding for Transgressors,' 14.
36. Ibid., 'King and Priest,' 83-84.

people are gathered in worship, he may pass by them to heal and to restore. The three invocations, then, are thoughtfully allocated. They are appropriate to our experience in salvation of an attentive Father, an alighting Spirit, and a Son who frequently visits us in mercy and power.

Distinct communion derives its vitality from beholding the persons in their saving roles. That point was argued in the previous chapter, and it is borne out in the prayers of Charles Spurgeon. He has particular things to say to each person because of each person's particular contribution to redemption. His person-specific adoration never feels forced or contrived. He is never scraping the barrel. He does not come up with highly generic petitions and then haphazardly attach to different ones the different persons' names. Rather, he has always before his eyes the great story of the gospel with its three magnificent characters; and that story organically and irrepressibly floods his prayers with distinct material reserved for each of them. It is clear from Spurgeon that the practice of pervasive Trinitarian prayer begins with immersion in a pervasively Trinitarian gospel.

Exploration

'Prayer,' says Robert Letham, 'is…exploration of the Holy Trinity.'[37] That is an attractive description. Perhaps our failure to perceive prayer as an exciting venture into 'the land of the Trinity'[38] explains why so many of us do so little of it! The believer in prayer is invited to go exploring. However, it is not pioneering exploration into uncharted territory. There

---

37. Robert Letham, *The Holy Trinity: In Scripture, History, Theology, and Worship* (Phillipsburg, N.J.: P&R Publishing, 2004), 422.

38. C.S. Lewis' intriguing phrase (C.S. Lewis, *The Four Loves* [London: HarperCollins*Publishers*, 1977], 116).

is a map. That map is the biblical narrative of redemption. As we scrutinise its lines and contours, we see the redeeming Father; then, as we continue to gaze, the redeeming Son comes into view; soon, the redeeming Spirit is just as clearly apparent.

To explorers a map is an invitation. Its depiction of a hill over here, and a valley over there, is an irresistible invitation to *climb* the hill and *descend* the valley. Similarly, in prayer the believer launches into the terrain delineated so alluringly on her map. She explores the Father, the Son and the Spirit. Having learnt from studying the gospel who these persons are, she proceeds to experience them for herself.

It is my hope that readers of this book will wish to be such explorers. James Durham's unease ought not to deter us. Instead, we should be inspired by Gregory Nazianzen's relish and Charles Spurgeon's spiritedness — or, indeed, by the simple but refreshing Trinitarian explorations of more recent figures:

Good morning heavenly Father, good morning Lord Jesus, good morning Holy Spirit.

Heavenly Father, I worship you as the creator and sustainer of the universe. Lord Jesus, I worship you, Saviour and Lord of the world. Holy Spirit, I worship you, sanctifier of the people of God.

Glory to the Father, and to the Son and to the Holy Spirit.

Heavenly Father, I pray that I may live this day in your presence and please you more and more. Lord Jesus, I pray that this day I may take up my cross and follow you. Holy Spirit, I pray that this day you will fill me with yourself and cause your fruit to ripen in my life: Love, joy, peace, patience, kindness, goodness, faithfulness, gentleness and self-control.

Holy, blessed, and glorious Trinity, three persons in one God, have mercy upon me.

Amen.[39]

* * *

Father almighty, maker of heaven and earth:
Set up your kingdom in our midst.
Lord Jesus Christ, Son of the living God:
Have mercy on me, a sinner.
Holy Spirit, breath of the living God:
Renew me and all the world.[40]

---

39. The prayer which, apparently, John Stott offered every morning (Roger Steer, *Basic Christian: The Inside Story of John Stott* [Leicester: Inter-Varsity Press, 2010], 246-47).

40. This prayer is proposed by N.T. Wright and discussed at length in, N.T. Wright, *New Tasks for a Renewed Church* (London: Hodder, 1992), 209-15.

CHAPTER SEVEN

Praying to the Holy Spirit

'Prayer,' says Kelly Kapic, 'is the appointed means of maintaining communion with God'.[1] Of course, the other 'means of grace' are also relevant to communion. But prayer is the obvious area in which the distinct communion of this book comes into play. It is to this particular devotional activity that, in our interactions with James Durham and Charles Spurgeon, we have naturally gravitated.

For some, however, as soon as communion is linked closely to prayer, there arises a problem with distinct communion.

---

1. Kelly M. Kapic, *Communion with God: The Divine and the Human in the Theology of John Owen* (Grand Rapids, Michigan: Baker Academic, 2007), 201. Cf. Warfield: 'The sacred idea of prayer *per se* is ... to put it sharply, just communion with God, the meeting of the soul with God, and the holding of converse with Him ... conscious communion with Him is just prayer' (B.B. Warfield, *Faith and Life* [Edinburgh: Banner of Truth, 1974], 152). And John Owen, writing of prayer to the Spirit — the very matter to which we are about to turn — remarks: 'In our prayers to him ... lies our communion with him' (John Owen, *Of Communion with God the Father, Son, and Holy Ghost, Each Person Distinctly, in Love, Grace, and Consolation* [1657], in *The Works of John Owen*, ed. William H. Goold [Edinburgh: Banner of Truth, 2004], 2:271).

For communing distinctly with the Spirit thereby involves *praying to the Spirit*, and that to their minds is dubious. Every time I have spoken anywhere on the subject of tri-personal devotion I have been confronted with the question, 'Does that mean it is right to pray to the Spirit?'

Though so commonly asked, the question still surprises me. It does so for a couple of reasons. First, our evangelical forebears betray no unease about this practice. John Owen, for instance, did not leave praying to the Spirit as something which the occasional, more adventurous reader might infer from his Trinitarian approach to communion. He is explicit on the matter:

> The distinction of the persons in the Trinity is not to be fancied, but believed. So, then, the Scripture so fully, frequently, clearly, distinctly ascribing the things we have been speaking of to the immediate efficiency of the Holy Ghost, faith closeth with him in the truth revealed, and peculiarly regards him, worships him, serves him, waits for him, prayeth to him, praiseth him ... Are not ... praises and blessings due to him by whom the work of redemption is made effectual to us? who with no less infinite love undertook our consolation than the Son our redemption. When we feel our hearts warmed with joy, supported in peace, established in our obedience, let us ascribe to him the praise that is due to him, bless his name and rejoice in him. And this glorifying of the Holy Ghost ... is no small part of our communion with him. Considering his free engagement in this work, his coming forth from the Father to this purpose, his mission by the Son, and condescension therein, his love and kindness, the soul of a believer is poured out in thankful praises to him, and is sweetly affected with the duty. There is no duty that leaves a more heavenly savour in the soul than this doth.[2]

---

2. Owen, *Works*, 2:270-71.

Moreover, James Durham, though so cautious in his general approach to Trinitarian prayer, has no reservations about the appropriateness of praying to the Spirit.[3] And Spurgeon, as we have seen, can, throughout a prolonged section of prayer, focus exclusively on the Spirit, directing one petition after another to this divine person.

Misgivings about this seem, then, to be a peculiarly modern phenomenon. The explanation for that — which cannot be explored in any depth here — probably relates to the rise of Pentecostalism. A perceived over-emphasis on the Spirit within that movement has engendered a wariness within the Reformed churches. Wishing to distance ourselves from a preoccupation with the Spirit's gifts and miracles, we have veered to the other extreme. The baby has been thrown out with the bathwater: a denial of certain activities commonly associated with the Spirit has morphed into a denial of anything that foregrounds this divine person. In the language of an earlier chapter, he has become solely a facilitator, never an object in his own right. Without us noticing, our relationship to the Spirit has been complicated by a raft of neuroses that would have baffled our heroes from the past.[4]

---

3. James Durham, *A Learned and Complete Commentary upon the Book of Revelation, Delivered in Several Lectures* (Glasgow: David Niven, 1788), 25-26.

4. George Smeaton's classic work on Pneumatology includes some brief but interesting reflections on Brethrenism. He contends that its members 'take exception to what other Churches...have always regarded as one of the most important and blessed duties.... The Church of God of all ages... — the Greek Church, the Roman Church, all the Protestant Churches... — have invoked the Holy Ghost...; and they grieve for and confess their sin in not having more implored His help and presence' (George Smeaton, *The Holy Spirit* [London: The Banner of Truth Trust, 1958], 356). If Smeaton's analysis is correct, it is possible that this movement's

The other reason the question surprises me is that those who ask it probably invoke the Spirit reasonably often themselves, only in a slightly different form. They do it in song! When we sing Elizabeth Head's 'O Breath of Life Come Sweeping Through Us,' James Montgomery's 'O Spirit of the Living God,' or Charles Wesley's 'Spirit of Faith, Come Down,' we are unambiguously calling upon the Spirit. Yet I have never heard anyone question the propriety of singing such lyrics. There is no obvious reason why sung prayers to the Spirit should be less problematic than unsung ones. It is a strange inconsistency.

But, of course, the fact that this question surprises me is immaterial. A concern about praying to the Spirit is clearly present in the minds of many, and so it ought not to be dismissed out of hand. Indeed, there are a couple of theological assertions to which that concern can plausibly attach itself. To those we must now give some attention.

The Bible Offers No Precedent for Praying to the Spirit

In the New Testament there are prayers addressed to the Father and there are prayers addressed to the Lord Jesus. There are prayers, as we saw in chapter three, addressed to the one God who is Father, Son and Spirit. But there are no prayers that use pneumatological vocatives like those we encountered in Spurgeon ('Divine Spirit'; 'Sweet Spirit'). In the absence, then, of any examples from the apostles and the first Christian churches, it might appear reckless to direct our intercessions to the Spirit.

However, given that the New Testament writings are, in Warfield's words, 'occasional in their origin and practical

---

aversion to invoking the Spirit has over time spread beyond its borders and influenced other strands of evangelicalism.

rather than doctrinal in their immediate purpose,'[5] it is questionable whether our theology of prayer should be dictated by the actual examples of prayer that we are given. Luke recorded in Acts the prayers that happened to be offered at certain key moments in the first Christian decades; Paul interjected prayers in his epistles consonant with the themes he happened to be treating. Neither writer was intending to lay down a definitive template from which Christians must never deviate in their prayers.

Actually, the New Testament does not feature an abundance of prayers addressed to the Son, either. The dying Stephen cries out, 'Lord Jesus' (Acts 7:59), Paul exclaims 'Our Lord, come!' (1 Cor. 16:22), and one or two other prayers probably, if not categorically, intend Christ as their recipient (e.g. Acts 1:24-25). It is not an extensive collection. And yet at several points the New Testament effectively defines Christianity in terms of calling on the name of the Lord Jesus. Paul refers to 'all those who in every place call upon the name of our Lord Jesus Christ' (1 Cor. 1:2). Again, he states that 'everyone who calls on the name of the Lord will be saved' (Rom. 10:13). In Acts 9:14 Ananias tells Jesus that Saul of Tarsus 'has authority from the chief priests to bind all who call on your name.' According to Acts 22:14-16 Ananias informed Saul that the latter's encounter on the Damascus Road had been with the Righteous One, before then instructing Saul to 'be baptised and wash away your sins, calling on his name.' The eighteenth- and nineteenth-century Baptist theologian Andrew Fuller comments on this material:

---

5. B.B. Warfield, 'The Biblical Doctrine of the Trinity,' in *Biblical and Theological Studies*, ed. Samuel G. Craig (Philadelphia, Pennsylvania: Presbyterian and Reformed, 1968), 36.

These modes of expression (which if I be not greatly mistaken, always signify divine worship) plainly inform us, that it was not merely the practice of a few individuals, but of the great body of the primitive christians, to invoke the name of Christ; nay, and that this was a mark by which they were distinguished as christians.[6]

If calling upon Christ was the Christians' distinguishing mark, and yet in the New Testament we only rarely see them doing it, that suggests the examples we have are far from representative.

We do not, therefore, require a precedent to justify praying to the Spirit. We only require theological warrant. And that is to be found in the Spirit's unabbreviated deity. Durham expresses the matter succinctly: 'He that is God, may be invoked.' Again, he says of praying to the Spirit: 'The general commands of glorifying God, must infer so much, supposing the Spirit to be God.'[7] The idea of a divine person to whom adoration and intercession are not due is an absurdity. The impious may *blaspheme* the Spirit (Matt. 12:31); are we to suppose that the saints may not *petition* him?

A commitment to the Spirit's deity, then, ought to lead to him being invoked. But there may also be a very troubling converse: when the Spirit is not being invoked, commitment to his deity will wane. The defence of *Christ's* deity has always been driven by a profound existential motivation:

---

6. Andrew Fuller, *The Calvinistic and Socinian Systems Examined and Compared, as to Their Moral Tendency: In a Series of Letters, Addressed to the Friends of Vital and Practical Religion* (Boston: Lincoln & Edmands, 1815), 123. cf. John Murray: 'The mark of New Testament believers is that they call upon the name of the Lord Jesus' (John Murray, *Collected Writings of John Murray* Vol. 1 [Edinburgh: The Banner of Truth Trust, 1989], 167).

7. Durham, *Revelation*, 25-26.

as Christians, we worship him; we *need*, therefore, a divine Christ in order to absolve us from idolatry. If, however, we do not need a divine Spirit, because we do not worship him, we are left with little incentive to defend his deity. The ancient principle, *lex orandi legem statuat credendi* ('the rule of prayer establishes the rule of faith'), expresses that point. It is when great swathes of our liturgy and devotion are at stake that a theological truth becomes urgent. In itself the deity of the Spirit might be viewed as an abstract, irrelevant dogma. For the believer who daily prays to the Spirit, however, it cannot be that. For her the Spirit's deity means everything.

The Spirit Is an Intrinsically Unsuitable Recipient of Our Prayers

This is the other theological assertion that can accompany a reluctance to pray to the Spirit. It is a less concrete one. The absence of a biblical precedent is after all a sheer fact — even if, as I argued above, that fact has been misconstrued. The Spirit's unsuitableness to receive prayer, on the other hand, is an impression, a feeling, a sense.

Perhaps it has to do with nomenclature. Our favourite designation for this divine person appears to be 'Spirit,' and our second favourite, 'Breath' — popularised by, for example, Elizabeth Head's hymn mentioned above. Such designations portray him as passive, someone who merely lurks in the background. They do not encourage us to give attention to him and seek a relationship with him. This can be demonstrated from some comments Hans Urs von Balthasar makes about the Spirit as *breath*:

> [The] Spirit is breath, not a full outline, and therefore he wishes only to breathe through us, not to present himself to us as an object; he does not wish to be seen but to be the seeing eye of grace in us, and he is little concerned about

whether we pray to him, provided that we pray *with* him, 'Abba, Father', provided that we consent to his unutterable groaning in the depths of our soul.[8]

For Balthasar it is almost axiomatic that, being but *breath*, this person is not the object of our prayers.

'Spirit' and 'Breath' are not incorrect titles. They do belong within the range of nuances that the Hebrew term *ruach* and the Greek term *pneuma* have. Indeed, there are biblical texts where 'Spirit' or 'Breath' captures very well the way that this person is being portrayed (cf., respectively, 1 Cor. 2:10-16 and John 20:22). It is unfortunate, however, that a key nuance of the terms *ruach* and *pneuma* is often overlooked: this divine person is also *the Wind*! There is nothing passive and lurking about a mighty hurricane in full force, and that is how the Scriptures often wish us to perceive the *ruach/pneuma* of God. According to J.I. Packer:

> The picture is of air made to move vigorously, even violently, and the thought that the picture expresses is of energy let loose, executive force invading, power in exercise, life demonstrated by activity.[9]

It is consistent with this idea of *violent power* that to this divine person are attributed some of God's most startling exploits — adorning the sky with its countless stars (Job 26:13), expelling demons (Matt. 12:28), raising the dead (1 Pet. 3:18; Rom. 8:11), and transforming the hearts of formerly depraved men and women (Eph. 3:16), to name a few! One wonders what more he would need to do to convince Balthasar that he is 'a full outline'! The dynamic, hyperactive

---

8. Hans Urs von Balthasar, *Explorations in Theology*, vol. 3, *Creator Spirit* (San Francisco: Ignatius Press, 1993), 111.

9. J.I. Packer, *Keep in Step with the Spirit* (Leicester: Inter-Varsity Press, 1984), 57.

Wind of God depicted in the Bible is a much more obvious object of prayer than the lacklustre *breath* imagined by the Swiss theologian.

But nomenclature does not seem to be the only reason the Spirit's suitability to receive prayers has been questioned. A couple of his *activities* also have a bearing. According to T.F. Torrance, the Spirit 'effaces himself in his very mode of Activity as Spirit'.[10]

Interceding Before the Father and Glorifying Christ

Balthasar, of course, is correct that the Spirit plays an important role in our prayers *to the other persons*. Paul does indeed present him as an intercessor whose prayers to the Father *for us* somehow accompany and elucidate our own inadequate requests (Rom. 8:26-27). Does that not settle, then, the issue of how the Spirit relates to prayer? Surely, his role is at the *offering* end rather than at the *receiving* end!

But to draw that inference from Romans 8 is to make an assumption: the Spirit must be *either* an intercessor *or* a recipient of intercession. But why can he not be both? Is that a logical impossibility? Paul prayed to Christ (1 Cor. 16:22) while at the same time deriving comfort from his intercessions at the Father's right hand (Rom. 8:34). Few of us, I suspect, struggle with that tension. And there is no reason we should struggle to conceive of the Spirit in a similarly dual way. We saw in chapter two that this is how communion with the triune God works: the persons all act as both facilitators and objects; each has his own direct engagement with the believer, while also effecting the engagement with the believer which the others have.

---

10. Thomas F. Torrance, *Theology in Reconstruction* (Eugene, Oregon: Wipf & Stock Publishers, 1996), 252.

But there is another work of the Spirit which, even more than his ministry of intercession, gets pitted against the idea of him receiving prayer. Jesus says of the Spirit in John 16:14: 'He will glorify me.' On the basis of this text, the attempt to glorify the Spirit, by directing adoring prayers to him, is seen by some as a tragic irony. It is perceived as badly missing the point — focusing on this person (the Spirit) who in fact is trying to ensure all the focus goes on a different person (the Son)! According to Packer, the Spirit is 'the hidden floodlight shining on the Saviour.'[11] No sane person seeks out a hidden floodlight, and harbours an equal admiration for *it* as for the object of its beams! Surely, if he is Christ's glorifier, then Colin Gunton is right: 'It is not in every way a bad thing that we do not speak much about the Spirit.'[12]

That mindset, it seems, has always asserted itself when attempts have been made to foreground the Spirit. Or at least, since the fourth century it has. For in his introduction to *De Spiritu Sancto*, Basil the Great explains the reason for writing this pneumatological work:

Lately when praying with the people, and using the full doxology to God the Father in both forms, at one time *with* the Son *together with* the Holy Ghost, and at another *through* the Son *in* the Holy Ghost, I was attacked by some of those present on the ground that I was introducing novel and at the same time mutually contradictory terms.[13]

The attacks related to the first form of the doxology that he mentions: the formula, 'with the Holy Ghost.' To Basil's

---

11. Packer, op. cit., 66.

12. Colin E. Gunton, *Father, Son and Holy Spirit: Toward a Fully Trinitarian Theology* (London: T & T Clark, 2003), 80.

13. Basil, *De Spiritu Sancto* 1.3, in *The Nicene and Post-Nicene Fathers*, vol. 8, ed. Philip Schaff and Henry Wace (Grand Rapids, Michigan: Wm. B. Eerdmans Publishing Company, 1978).

detractors, glorifying the other persons 'in the Holy Ghost' was appropriate and consonant with his Johannine role. Including him among those glorified, on the other hand, conflicted with that. As far as they were concerned, we cannot offer worship through the Spirit's enabling and then in the same breath make him an object of our worship!

But these treatments of Jesus' words are highly unsatisfactory. Apart from anything else, they ignore the context of the statement in John 16. Jesus is in the upper room addressing the twelve. Here are verses 12-14 in full:

> I still have many things to say to you, but you cannot bear them now. When the Spirit of truth comes, he will guide you into all the truth, for he will not speak on his own authority, but whatever he hears he will speak, and he will declare to you the things that are to come. He will glorify me, for he will take what is mine and declare it to you.

These men had the role of authoritatively bearing witness to the truth following Christ's ascension (John 19:35; 21:24). Jesus' promise is that the Spirit will enable them to fulfil that role. It is in that context, specifically, that he will glorify Christ. Jesus does not have in mind the new covenant period generally. He has in mind a fixed period during which the apostles will articulate definitively the truth on which the church is to be founded (Eph. 2:20). Because of the Spirit, they will not make a mess of that task. Their faulty memories and weak comprehension will not impair their work, so that the greatness and beauty of Christ are inadequately conveyed, and the Christian church made to rest on a flimsy foundation. No, Jesus says, the Spirit will glorify me, for he will take what is mine and declare it to you.

But, more importantly, withholding glory from the Spirit because he is a glorifier involves the same fallacy as withholding intercession from the Spirit because he is an intercessor. Why should the work of giving glory to another preclude a divine person from simultaneously receiving glory himself? Packer's floodlight analogy is unhelpful. Of course, an inanimate structure of metal, glass and electrical wiring is an unsuitable object of admiration! Of course, it is deliberately 'hidden' out of sight. Of course, it performs an entirely one-way role — always giving, never receiving. But the Spirit is not an inanimate structure of metal, glass and wiring! He floodlights but he is not a floodlight. He is himself a Magnificence comparable with the Magnificence he illumines.

A few verses after Jesus' statement about the Spirit, he begins his famous 'high-priestly' prayer. Its opening petition is: 'Father, the hour has come; glorify your Son that the Son may glorify you' (John 17:1). That line makes it clear that, actually, being a glorifier does not distinguish the Spirit from the other two persons. They are all glorifiers! As William Hendriksen puts it: 'There exists between the persons of the Trinity an eternal…relationship of love and friendship, each working for the glory and honour of the others.'[14] Thus, if giving glory precludes receiving glory, there are no divine persons left to whom we may adoringly pray! In that case they are all self-effacing, all averse to too much attention! It is a ludicrous state of affairs.

But we must eschew such madness. We must understand, rather, that all the divine persons glorify, and all the divine persons are to be glorified. It is not otherwise with the Spirit.

---

14. William Hendriksen, *A Commentary on the Gospel of John* (London: Banner of Truth, 1964), 329. Commendably, it is in his comments on John 16:14 itself that Hendriksen makes this remark. He has escaped the gravitational pull of the text's common interpretation.

He is not in a different category than the other two. There is not in his case a complication excluding him from some of their prerogatives. Nothing about his particular identity, or his particular activity, places him off-limits as a recipient of prayer. Sinclair Ferguson laments what he terms 'a significant hiatus in discussions of the Spirit.' He continues:

> It is commonplace to discuss the question of his divine personhood, his work in the application of redemption and in the fruit he produces, or the nature of his gifts and their role in the contemporary church; but communion with him in a developing knowledge of him is much less frequently explored. It might be thought that this hiatus has solid biblical foundations. After all, the Spirit does not draw attention to himself; he has even been referred to as the 'shy' member of the Trinity. His task is to glorify Christ, not to speak of or draw attention to himself (*cf.* John 16:13-15). But to draw the conclusion from this that we should not focus our attention on the Spirit ... or grow in personal knowledge of him, is a mistake ... He is to be glorified together with the Father and the Son.[15]

The Spirit and Salvation

At the beginning of the chapter, I quoted Owen on the propriety and importance of praying to the Spirit. His approach to this specific matter is consistent with his approach to distinct communion generally. We saw in chapter five his pivotal insight that each divine person has contributed his own activities to our salvation, and that 'in these things is the person ... proposed unto us to be known and adored.'[16] Our communion with each is not directionless

---

15. Sinclair B. Ferguson, *The Holy Spirit* (Downers Grove, Illinois: Inter-Varsity Press, 1996), 185-86.

16. John Owen, *A Discourse Concerning the Holy Spirit* (1674), in *The Works of John Owen*, ed. William H. Goold (Edinburgh:

and arbitrary. Rather, it focuses on that person's role within salvation. And Owen's remarks on praying to the Spirit are true to that principle. The believer, getting down on her knees and starting to address the Spirit, does not receive from Owen a tabula rasa. She is directed by the Puritan to the Spirit's saving work. It is in the light of Scripture ascribing things 'to the immediate efficiency of the Holy Ghost' that 'faith closeth with him in the truth revealed, and peculiarly regards him, worships him, serves him, waits for him, prayeth to him, praiseth him.' It is 'considering his free engagement in this work...[that] the soul of a believer is poured out in thankful praises to him'.[17]

And Owen had a particularly expansive understanding of the Spirit's 'engagement in this work'. This fact doubtless contributes to his relish for prayer-communion with the Spirit. In respect of this divine person, many of us, I suspect, struggle to find 'devotional anchor-points'[18] within salvation's storyline. The Spirit after all did not sacrifice his Son for us. He did not become incarnate and die on a cross. We make a text like 1 Peter 1:2 definitive for our understanding of tri-personal salvation. There the Father is linked with 'foreknowledge' and the Son with 'blood.' The 'sanctification' which Peter ascribes to the Spirit could appear by comparison small-scale and limited. There is little, we might feel, that our prayers can fasten on as we invoke this divine person.

Owen clearly had no sense of that. This is partly because he regarded sanctification itself as a grand thing: 'It is a

Banner of Truth, 2004), 3:159.

17. Owen, *Works*, 2:270-71 (italics mine).

18. The phrase is Brian Kay's (Brian Kay, *Trinitarian Spirituality: John Owen and the Doctrine of God in Western Devotion* [Milton Keynes: Paternoster, 2007], 41).

greater matter to be truly and really holy than most persons are aware of ... It [is] of great importance unto the glory of God, so of an eminent nature in itself.'[19] And within this grand project of sanctification, he perceived the Spirit as a ubiquitous, hands-on, comprehensively involved agent:

> The actual aid, assistance, and internal operation of the Spirit of God is necessary, required, and granted, unto the producing of every holy act of our minds, wills, and affections, in every duty whatever;...notwithstanding the power or ability which believers have received in or by habitual grace, they still stand in need of actual grace, in, for, and unto every single gracious, holy act or duty towards God.[20]

Thus, the Spirit's sanctifying ministry alone, being so glorious in its outcome and so manifold in its operations, affords 'devotional anchor-points' aplenty.

But another factor is worth noting. Owen did not confine the Spirit's redemptive contribution to sanctification. Indeed, he did not confine it to the *ordo salutis*. In Owen's soteriology the Spirit was highly active in the *historia salutis*: in the preparatory era of the old covenant; and, especially, in the mission of the Son. The Spirit created the Son's human nature

---

19. Owen, *Works*, 3:481.

20. Ibid., 3:529. The 'habitual grace' to which Owen refers is the regenerate state effected by the Spirit at the inception of the Christian life. 'Actual grace,' on the other hand, is his particular enabling of each holy action performed within that regenerate state. Owen laments, almost sardonically, the hubris which downplays this moment by moment grace on which our holy conduct depends: 'It is hard to persuade, with many, that [the Spirit] continues now to do almost any good at all; and what he is allowed to have any hand in, it is sure to be so stated as that the principal praise of it may redound unto ourselves. So diverse, yea, so adverse, are the thoughts of God and men in these things' (ibid., 3:151).

in the virgin's womb. He empowered Christ's miracles. He granted Christ's mind revelation. He enabled Christ's spoken ministry, so that 'he continually on all occasions put forth his wisdom, power, grace, and knowledge, to the astonishment of all, and the stopping of the mouths of his adversaries'.[21] He shaped Christ's character, so that there was a 'perfection and fulness of grace which dwelt in his human nature, as communicated unto him by the Holy Spirit'.[22] He 'guided, directed, comforted, supported [Christ] in the whole course of his ministry, temptations, obedience, and sufferings.'[23] He raised Christ from the dead on Easter Sunday morning.

In attributing so much of the Son's mission to the work of the Spirit, Owen was driven partly by explicit biblical data but also by the theological concern to defend the authenticity of the incarnation. He refused to accept that as the man, Jesus, went about on this earth, his 'divine nature…did immediately operate the things which he performed, as some of old vainly imagined'.[24] That would involve a 'transfusion of the properties of one nature into the other'.[25] Christ's humanity, benefitting so freely from his divinity, would thereby not be comparable to our own. Owen could not countenance that. He insisted, instead, that 'the only singular immediate act of the person of the Son on the human nature was the assumption of it into subsistence with himself.'[26] Once that assumption had occurred, 'all the…communications of the divine nature unto the human were…by the Holy Spirit'[27] — just as they are for us.

---

21. Ibid., 3:175.
22. Ibid., 3:188.
23. Ibid., 3:174.
24. Ibid., 3:169.
25. Ibid., 3:161.
26. Ibid., 3:160.
27. Ibid., 3:175.

Driven, then, by these concerns, Owen ends up with a remarkably wide-ranging pneumatology. The Spirit does not suddenly enter the story of redemption on the day of Pentecost! Indeed, for Owen it is impossible to view the Son's saving work without at the same time observing the Spirit in action. He writes:

> Would you, therefore, propose Christ unto your affections, so as that your love unto him may be sincere and without corruption ...? — consider his human nature, as it was rendered beautiful and lovely by the work of the Spirit of God upon it ... Do you love him because he was and is so full of grace, so full of holiness, because in him there was an all-fulness of the graces of the Spirit of God? ... If we love the person of Christ, it must be on these considerations.[28]

Within the very anchor points of our devotion to the Son, we encounter anchor points for our devotion to the Spirit! The believer who appreciates this will never be short of matters about which to speak to the Spirit. The riches of his ministry within our own lives already yield abundant material. His role in the Son's mission opens vast, additional storehouses which the saint, praying to the Spirit, may eagerly ransack!

'Who with the Father and the Son Together is Worshipped and Glorified'

Mention was made earlier in the chapter of Basil the Great's doxological formula: worshipping the Father 'with the Son together with the Holy Ghost'. Though criticised by his contemporaries, the formula soon took root. The Constantinopolitan revision of the Nicene Creed (381), written two years after Basil's death, included the very similar words: 'And in the Holy Ghost, the Lord and Giver

---

28. Ibid., 3:187-188.

151

of life, who proceedeth from the Father, who with the Father and the Son together is worshipped and glorified.'

The issue of praying to the Spirit was thus resolved in the church in the fourth century. It is disappointing that this practice should sometimes raise eyebrows among orthodox Christians nearly seventeen hundred years later! We appear to have regressed. John James is right: in a stimulating article on the Spirit as *homotimia* (equal in honour), and the triumph of that concept in fourth-century Christianity, he concludes, 'A good dose of the Niceno-Constantinopolitan creed may be just the tonic to relieve our current pneumatological blindness in theology and worship'! [29]

Whether it is that ancient creed — or the writings of John Owen, or the prayers of Charles Spurgeon — may the triune God indeed use something to remove every form of blindness that keeps us from communing distinctly with Father, Son and Spirit.

---

29.   John L.W. James, 'An Examination of *Homotimia* in St. Basil the Great's *On the Holy Spirit*, and Contemporary Implications,' *Westminster Theological Journal* 74 (2012): 276. James is critical of the approach to the Spirit that is solely interested in the concept of *homoousia* (equal in essence). For Basil (and others who influenced the creedal revision), 'The imperative throughout is doxological' (ibid., 263). Indeed, as I signalled earlier in the chapter, without a passion for the Spirit as *homotimia*, there is little reason to be interested in the Spirit as *homoousia*.

Conclusion

Our 'chief end' as human beings, the Westminster Shorter Catechism insists, is 'to glorify God, and to enjoy him for ever.' If that is true, then we ought to think rigorously about how we are to go about glorifying and enjoying God.

This book is intended to help with that. Its aim is not the imposition of rigid rules and formulae to which every act of Christian devotion must conform. Its aim is simply to encourage believers to think more about their communion with God.

Hopefully, those readers who regularly lead corporate acts of worship will especially be stimulated to think. Perhaps they will be inspired to ask the question, 'What kinds of songs and prayers will most enable this congregation to commune distinctly with the different divine persons?' Of course, some who lead worship may not quite be ready for such a thoroughgoing implementation of the ideas in this book. But if the foregoing pages at least cause words like 'God' and 'Lord' to be used with a more developed Trinitarian consciousness, that itself is a gain worth making.

However, the individual believer, too – not just the professional concerned with liturgy – is being invited to think. Every Christian believes in the doctrine of the Trinity. Every Christian understands the gospel to be the story of three agents fulfilling different saving roles. But many struggle to assimilate that belief and that understanding into their daily relationship with God. This brief treatment of distinct communion is an exhortation to readers to 'join the dots'; to be Trinitarian experientially as well as credally; to distinguish between Father, Son and Spirit in the realm of devotion no less than in the realm of salvation.

And to sound once more a note which I hope has been discerned already, the potential rewards for doing this thinking are great. Distinct communion does not complicate and clutter the business of knowing God. It enriches it. It opens up magnificent new dimensions and possibilities. Here, three divine persons, each one eternally and irreducibly unique, confront us, all of them infinitely beautiful and praiseworthy. We dance between them, tasting the joys of the One who died for us; then luxuriating in the pleasures of the One who adopted us; then basking in the delights of the One in whom we have been baptised. We address to each such words as particularly are due to that person. To grapple thus with 'the splendour of the three' is to experience intimacy with God in its most exquisite form.

We must not confine the doctrine of the Trinity to our doorsteps, as merely an argument to pick when the Jehovah's Witnesses visit. We must bring it into our homes and into our lives and into our churches. It must shape everything, and not least the way that we relate to God. When that is truly happening, the result will be distinct communion. May it be so!

Also available from Christian Focus Publications ...

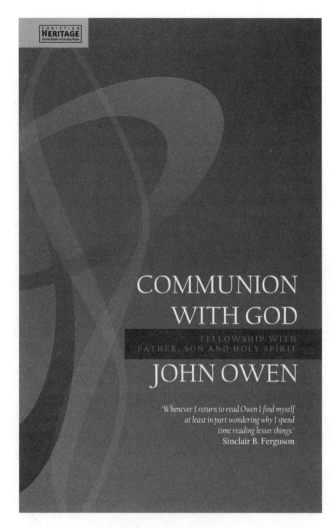

COMMUNION
WITH GOD

FELLOWSHIP WITH
FATHER, SON AND HOLY SPIRIT

JOHN OWEN

'Whenever I return to read Owen I find myself
at least in part wondering why I spend
time reading lesser things.'
Sinclair B. Ferguson

978-1-84550-209-6

COMMUNION WITH GOD

Fellowship with the Father, Son and Holy Spirit

JOHN OWEN

In 1657, John Owen produced one of his finest devotional treatises: probably originating from the substance of a series of sermons.

He examines the Christian's communion with God as it relates to all three members of the trinity. He assures that every Christian does have communion with God, no-one is excluded and that this communion takes place distinctly with Father, Son and Holy Spirit. Our relationship with…

God the Father is primarily through love and faith.

God the Son is through fellowship & grace.

God the Holy Spirit is primarily through comfort and sanctification.

I owe an incalculable debt to these pages. For forty years now this has been a favourite volume to which I continue to return for more 'angel food.'

SINCLAIR B. FERGUSON
Teaching Fellow, Ligonier Ministries

THE TRINITY AND THE
FELLOWSHIP OF GOD'S PEOPLE

30th
Anniversary Edition

Shared Life

Donald Macleod

978-1-5271-1069-4

SHARED LIFE

The Trinity and the Fellowship of God's People

DONALD MACLEOD

Donald Macleod argues that our understanding of the Trinity matters because 'it is the model for the way we should live, particularly in our relations with one another.' The relationship between Father, Son and Spirit is laid out in Scripture, and although fully grasping the concept of this divine mystery will always be beyond us, we can understand it better. It is critically important that we do, for if our understanding of God is wrong, it may lead to other wrong beliefs.

Donald Macleod's faithful insight into what Scripture has to say about the Godhead is priceless, as relevant now as when it was first published. This 30th anniversary edition has been newly typeset and has a new cover, and will be an invaluable resource to a new generation of readers.

> The Christian doctrine of the Holy Trinity ... is one of the most precious truths on which a believer may meditate. For the beginner, *Shared Life* provides the ideal introduction.
>
> LIGON DUNCAN
> Reformed Theological Seminary,
> Jackson, Mississippi

Christian Focus Publications

Our mission statement
Staying Faithful

In dependence upon God we seek to impact the world through literature faithful to His infallible Word, the Bible. Our aim is to ensure that the Lord Jesus Christ is presented as the only hope to obtain forgiveness of sin, live a useful life and look forward to heaven with Him.

Our Books are published in four imprints:

◁◯╳ CHRISTIAN FOCUS

Popular works including biographies, commentaries, basic doctrine and Christian living.

◁◯╳ MENTOR

Books written at a level suitable for Bible College and seminary students, pastors, and other serious readers. The imprint includes commentaries, doctrinal studies, examination of current issues and church history.

◁◯╳ CHRISTIAN HERITAGE

Books representing some of the best material from the rich heritage of the church.

◁◯╳ CF4KIDS

Children's books for quality Bible teaching and for all age groups: Sunday school curriculum, puzzle and activity books; personal and family devotional titles, biographies and inspirational stories – because you are never too young to know Jesus!

Christian Focus Publications Ltd,
Geanies House, Fearn, Ross-shire,
IV20 1TW, Scotland, United Kingdom.
www.christianfocus.com